Saving,
Spending,
Investing,
Giving

Saving, Spending, Investing, Giving

A VETERAN
INVESTMENT ADVISOR
REFLECTS ON MONEY

Daniel Pecaut

Second Printing: 2018

Pecaut & Company
401 Douglas St #415
Sioux City, IA 51101

www.DanielPecaut.com

www.Pecautandcompany.com

CONTENTS

INTRODUCTION   1

PART 1
BUILDING A SOLID FOUNDATION FOR WEALTH
9

MONEY IS A TOOL   13

OPPORTUNITY COST   19

THE POWER OF COMPOUNDING   21

HOW MUCH TIME DO YOU HAVE?   27

DON'T LOSE   29

HOW TO HOLD ON TO YOUR MONEY   33

CHOOSING YOUR PATH AS AN INVESTOR   37

LEVELS OF WEALTH BUILDING   41

ACTION STEPS: PART ONE   45

PART 2
MAXIMIZING RETURNS: THINKING LIKE AN ENTREPRENEURIAL INVESTOR
47

DEVELOPING CLEAR THINKING   51

BECOMING A BUSINESS ANALYST   55

ACCOUNTING: THE LANGUAGE OF BUSINESS   57

WHAT IT TAKES TO GROW   61

HUNTING FOR TALENT   63

THE OWNERSHIP SHORTCUT   65

A CASE STUDY IN EXCELLENCE: NESTLÉ   71

THE MANIC DEPRESSIVE PSYCHOLOGY OF THE MARKET   73

TAKING MR. MARKET'S TEMPERATURE   77

DON'T LOSE (PART 2): WHAT COULD GO WRONG?   83

CONTROLLED GREED: PATIENCE IS THE VIRTUE   91

BARGAIN HUNTING: SEARCHING FOR TREASURE   97

ACTION STEPS: PART TWO   101

PART 3
HEAD & HEART:
GIVING WITH A BUSINESS MINDSET
105

JOHN TEMPLETON TOLD ME TO TITHE   109

BECOMING LESS ATTACHED TO MY GROWING WEALTH   111

SMALL GIFTS, LARGE IMPACT   113

MY FIRST LARGE GIFT: THE DOROTHY PECAUT
NATURE CENTER   115

MEASURING FOR MAXIMUM IMPACT   117

GOODWILL: AN ENTREPRENEURIAL NON-PROFIT   119

THE MANKIND PROJECT: AN ORGANIZATION
ON THE ROPES   125

PINE RIDGE: MAKING OF ALLIES   131

ACTION STEPS: BOOK THREE   137

PROCEEDS: HEALING THE
WOUNDS OF GENOCIDE   139

ACKNOWLEDGMENTS   141

APPENDIX I: FURTHER READING   143

INTRODUCTION

At first, I bought the idea that not everyone could save. Making ends meet is tough. Maybe "buy now, pay later" was the only way to go for some people. After reflecting on this issue, though, I've realized that saving has little to do with money. It has far more to do with attitude, discipline, and a willingness to rewire the circuits.

A former Peace Corps volunteer proved this to me when he told me this story:

> Some years ago, a family in India lived in conditions that, while destitute by our standards, were average for their neighborhood. They had a one-room shack that housed grandparents, parents, and five children.
>
> This Peace Corps volunteer noticed that the mother, as a mealtime tradition, would throw an extra handful of rice into the pot in case company came by for dinner. This was a beautiful gesture of hospitality and generosity. But company hardly ever came. The volunteer gently suggested that the mother save this extra handful of rice by throwing it into a bucket.
>
> Slowly, the bucket filled, and when it reached the brim, he took her to the marketplace and helped her sell the rice.
>
> This empowered mother decided she could get by with less if it meant a better future. With this discipline came empowerment. It offered her family hope and opportunity.
>
> When he visited a few years later, not only was this family continuing to save, they had taught their neighbors to save. They had founded a food cooperative. Each month, a member of the cooperative went to the big city and bought bulk quantities at wholesale prices for the group.

Saving has little to do with money. It has far more to do with attitude, discipline, and a willingness to change. Never have I found this point more eloquently put than in that story.

So saving isn't about the money. It's about building a future.

With this in mind, I want you to think of your life as an operation rather than an identity. In this operation, you're in charge. It isn't just day-to-day details like mowing the lawn and deciding what's for dinner. It's having a larger vision. Step back and ask, "How can I optimize my operation to routinely make high-quality choices so that, over time, my life gets better and better?"

Life rules are ingrained in us during our youth. As adults, we continue to make decisions based on these rules, until we stop to rewire the circuits. The first step in the rewiring process is to go back to the basics with money, look at how wealth is built, and set up a new blueprint for how to think about money. Then once you have a solid foundation, you can put it to maximum effect.

For most people, what they know about money comes from their parents. If their parents didn't know or share, then they don't know. Lucky for me, my parents did know.

I'm a third generation investor. My grandfather, father, and uncle were all in investing and together founded a firm, Pecaut & Company, in 1960.

There was a lot that was handed down. Even with this early advantage, however, it was a long road full of pitfalls for me to become a successful investor.

I graduated from Harvard in 1979 with a philosophy degree. While there, I took only one economics course. I found it too theoretical. It wasn't anything like the investing I saw happening in my family's business.

In the summers, I had worked at Pecaut & Company in the back office. I did the grunt work that needed to be done. One task was replacing S&P 500 tear sheets. The S&P had alphabetized encyclopedia-like binders. A packet would come in the mail with colored sheets that matched the binder. Green sheets were stocks. Yellow sheets were small stocks. Blue sheets were for bonds. When they arrived, someone needed to go in and take the old sheets out and put the new sheets in. I was just manually updating the binders. That was the job. But I learned about hundreds of businesses by readying those sheets.

Years later, I came to work full-time as an investor at Pecaut & Company. It was one of the most astonishing events in my whole life. I was 22 years old. I had just graduated from Harvard but my degree wasn't in any way related. I had studied philosophy. So I thought, "What am I doing? Who wants advice from me? I barely have my own budget. What do I have to offer?" I felt totally inadequate. I had no clue what I was doing. It wasn't like our small, family-run operation had a formal training program or structure. I felt isolated. My dad didn't sit me down in regular meetings to talk about how stuff was going with me. I tortured myself with my own self-judgment about how poorly I was doing. I tried to learn by showing up and paying attention. Needless to say, there was a lot of trial and error.

Before you invest, it's common to think investing consists of only one thing or that approaches are equally effective. Investing is taking your money and essentially trying to increase its value. But within that, the different schools can vary greatly. There are so many ways that people invest money—value investing, option trading strategies, growth investing, momentum investing, index hugging, and so on.

One error I made early on was with option trading. It was quick and exciting. You could, theoretically, triple your money in a short time period. If you hit with a few of those, you'd have a good year. I spent a year focused on seeing if I could figure out an option trading strategy. When the year was over, I had made about a hundred bucks. Calculated into the amount of time I spent, that's about 10 cents an hour. Clearly that wasn't worth it. Trading in the short term may work for some people, but it wasn't for me.

I needed a better way. I was ready for something.

In a desperate attempt to accelerate my learning process, I started calling local business owners. I thought, "Of all people, business owners would understand investing. When you buy a stock, you buy part ownership in a business. A person who fully owns a business must get this." But I was stunned to call on owner after owner who didn't know what a balance sheet was. They didn't know what their cash flow was. They didn't know if they were making money or losing money. They just had a vague feeling that things were "going pretty good."

I was absolutely stunned. It was a revelation. Here we are in the United States, the cradle of capitalism, where free enterprise has flourished for over 240 years, yet most U.S. citizens don't understand money.

Then in 1982, I read the book *The Money Masters* by John Train. In it, he profiles nine brilliant investors (including John Templeton and Warren Buffett). As I was finishing the book, the light bulb came on. I said, "I'm going back to school. These are my professors. My curriculum is anything they say or write." I was excited. I would study the most brilliant investors in the world like they were my professors at Harvard. I was on fire to learn everything I could about them and figure out how to be like them.

I took on a world-as-my-classroom approach to develop myself as an investor. I sought out outstanding individuals to use as my professors and did everything I could to learn from them. I started to see our firm primarily as a learning organism. The better we learn and think, the better our decision-making will be, and the better we will serve our clients.

My favorite professors were Sir John Templeton (of the Templeton Growth Fund), George Michaelis of Source Capital (a top performing closed-end fund), Jean-Marie Eveillard (who ran what is now the First Eagle Global Fund), Bob Rodriguez (of First Pacific Advisors), and Marty Whitman (of Third Avenue Value Investors). These people have given us tremendous insight and direction, but of all our brilliant "professors," no one has been more instructive than Berkshire Hathaway run by Warren Buffett and Charlie Munger.

After realizing that Warren Buffett was one of the guys to learn from, I read and ate up all his annual letters from Berkshire. Then I met a friend who had Buffett's letters from his partnership prior to Berkshire. Those were like gold. Every year since 1984, I've attended the Berkshire Hathaway meeting. When I started going, the meetings were so small that I could come up with a list of questions and directly ask Warren Buffett. Then in 1987, a group of investors and I traveled to Templeton's headquarters in the Bahamas to meet with John Templeton in person.

It quickly became clear that value investing was the approach that was going to underlie my career. It's not as quick or as dramatic as options trading. Yet I believe in value investing over the many other strategies because it works. It's worked for me for 30 years. Most of the other approaches just don't make a lot of sense. Value investing is about being as rational and clear each step of the way and owning great businesses. That makes sense to me.

I'm enamored with value investing, so I don't spend much time anymore thinking about a lot of other views. It's simple as a concept, but it's complex in execution. I like the simplicity of it. It's a clear but difficult road to take. I like the challenge of it. It's an approach that I can trust and believe in.

Why I Wrote This Book

I wrote this book for several reasons. One was a desire to summarize a life's worth of learning in my chosen field. I feel blessed to have had such great teachers, lessons, and opportunities come my way, and want to pass them along. In particular, I'd like to pass these insights along to the next generation, as it is today's 20- and 30-somethings that will be making the most important capital allocation decisions in the decades to come. This book is a legacy to my children and my children's generation.

I would like to improve financial literacy in the world. If people had the basic understanding of money and how money works—the lessons shared in this book—I believe civil society would operate at a more informed and effective level. It still surprises me that the citizens of America, the cradle of capitalism, are so significantly under-educated as to how money and finance actually work. This book is a small attempt on my part to improve financial literacy.

I also wrote this book to share a mindset that sees life as a learning laboratory. This has been an enormously helpful worldview for me. Everything that happens can carry a lesson within it. Seen this way, money is a fantastic teaching tool. As you use it in different ways (save, spend, invest, give), you will learn different life lessons. Learn the lessons and over time, you will develop better and better decision-making processes that will optimize your life's choices. Optimize your choices, optimize your life. (In Part Three, for example, I share how integrating head and heart with an investment mindset can bring outsized impacts in giving.)

In addition, I want to help you solve (or at least deal with) the complexity inherent in the world of money and finance.

You may already have an experienced advisor you trust. If so, well done. Maybe that's enough for you. On the other hand, the more you know, the more empowered your choices will be. I want you to know enough about money and finances to choose well. What I hope to give you in this book are the most essential elements to understand. With those under your belt, you'll be far better equipped to decide whether you want to go it alone or hire some help. And, if you hire help, you'll have a much better idea exactly what help you are looking and paying for.

Full disclosure: I run a registered investment advisory firm. Our firm is non-promotional (we have no marketing budget). We prefer for new clients to come to us by referral. The referrer helps both parties have a better idea of whether there is a fit. We are not for everyone. We have a clear investment philosophy, value investing, which is articulated and communicated via newsletters and client letters. Pecaut & Company was founded in 1960 by my grandfather, father and uncle. Together they instilled a culture of integrity in all dealings and an ethic of serving the client first. As a result, we have numerous decades-long relationships with our clients. I say this to give you a sense that you can trust what is shared in this book is solid insight and teaching. I'm glad to pass it along to you.

What This Book Is

This book is about core timeless principles and ways of thinking that will apply as much today as they will in 20 years.

This book is split up into three major subsections:

In Part One, I give a detailed but basic understanding of how to think about money. It covers the essentials you need to understand before you can go forward. I belabor a lot of points to set a solid foundation for you to build on. Part One is for everyone. There are valuable insights for everyone, no matter where you are in life. If you can understand and implement the concepts in this section, even if you skip the rest of the book, you will be well set up for financial success in life.

Part Two is an overview of the Entrepreneurial Investing process. If you want higher returns, invest the time and effort to master the skill set of the entrepreneurial investor. Part Two is for those who want to dig in and become business analysts. It's for those who probably found Part One a little too elementary. In Part Two, I start treating you more like an experienced investor.

I pull back to give you a wider picture. From this point forward, I don't try to give you exhaustive detail for every concept, but instead try to give you a full, robust picture of the investing landscape. There will be less detail about specifics and more broad strokes about how to think about your investments, how to set up an effective investment program, and how to structure your affairs. Because there are so many more details involved in this process than can be contained in this book, Part Two aims to give you an idea of what you need to know and how those factors interact with each other. There will be a lot of detail underneath these concepts.

If you get overwhelmed in the entrepreneurial investor section, skip ahead to Part Three: Head & Heart: Giving with a Business Mindset. Part Three is more of a memoir. I can't explain what your giving life will look like, so I only describe my own. This part is more personal and less didactic than the first two parts.

The Results You Can Expect From This Book

Most people have no idea how wealth building works. I wrote this book to help bridge that gap.

Proper money management is the only way to get control or freedom. It's a path to hope, possibility, and a brighter future. It's a path to creating the life you want.

Investing is the only way to maintain the value of your money against inflation. It's the only way to keep your money from diminishing over time.

With an understanding of money, the first thing you get is safety. It helps to let go of some of the worry around money. You're not on the razor's edge. Debt is a kind of negative wealth. Just getting to positive wealth is huge. Most people's net worth has a minus sign in front of it. To get to zero would be a huge step up.

If you have a large vision for your life with a sense of purpose and mission, money is a tool that gets things done. Your vision and your dreams can get constrained by the amount of capital that you have to work with. You have smaller, more attainable dreams in relation to smaller, available capital. With more capital, you have more options. That frees you up to have bigger dreams.

I want to give you a basic understanding of how money works and how you can use it to your advantage. This wider picture will inform your future development and create a strong framework to work within.

This book has been written for anyone, regardless of investing experience.

Becoming fluent and gaining mastery with money and investing is something anyone can do. They can learn how to handle their money with expertise, choose stocks, and watch the market.

With this, anyone can become a millionaire. As of 2013, roughly one out of every 100 people in America is a millionaire. You can be one, too.

It can be done. Most people probably could understand these key concepts in an hour or two. Then with some work, they could structure their lives so the concepts are operational the next day.

A result they can expect is to have their life structured in a way that helps optimize increasing their wealth while also protecting their wealth from loss. It optimizes their prospects for creating a more dynamic, economic life.

If your operation uses a better thinking process, your life will be much better. You'll make better decisions, large and small. You'll optimize those decisions more often than not. They won't all will work out, but as a percentage, you'll do increasingly better as you go. You'll live a fuller, more empowered, and meaningful life. You'll take control of your finances and steer your own course to investment success.

BUILDING A SOLID FOUNDATION FOR WEALTH

In Part One, I give a detailed but basic understanding of how to think about money.

It covers the essentials you need to understand before you can go forward. I belabor a lot of points to set a solid foundation for you to build on.

Part One is for everyone. There are valuable insights for everyone, no matter where you are in life.

If you can understand and implement the concepts in this section, even if you skip the rest of the book, you will be well set up for financial success in life.

Money Is a Tool

For most people, as I mentioned in the introduction, what they know about money comes from their parents. If their parents didn't know or share, then they don't know.

I'm grateful to my parents for the upbringing I had. They started me out early in life with an allowance. When I got a dollar, my mom made sure I put 10 cents in a little envelope that would later go in the collection plate at church. They also gave me a little piggy bank to put coins in. So the idea of giving and saving was instilled early.

At first, I felt a sting when I put money in the collection plate. I thought, "Aw, man. I worked hard for that dime." But when we got to church and that big heavy wooden plate was passed around, it felt good to contribute.

Before long, I happily and willingly gave my dime as I wanted to be part of what was happening. If I forgot to bring my dime to church, my mom would give me one, but it didn't feel the same. It felt like cheating. I knew it wasn't really my dime.

So, from an early stage, I understood that giving is a personal act. Saving is also very personal.

I had a little copper-colored cocker spaniel piggy bank. It had a slot for coins on the top of its head. I loved dropping coins in and hearing the clink, shaking it to see how heavy it was, and—not too often since I didn't want to spoil it—pulling the plug out to see how much money was inside. With this piggy bank, I became much more interested in saving than spending.

Growing up, I tried to figure out ways to slide by without spending. Although that has some value, it can also backfire.

I earned money with a paper route, shoveling snow in the winter, and mowing lawns in the summer. I also had special paid chores I could do to make money.

In my free time, I played basketball in our driveway. At one point, the black bladder inside the ball started to poke through the seams.

The ball became off center and wobbly when I shot it. So I thought, "I need a new basketball."

As I saved for a new ball, I would visit the sporting goods store and covet all the beautiful basketballs on display.

Once I had the money saved, though, I didn't want to spend it. I had worked too hard to earn and save the money. I decided I could get another year out of the ball.

When I was in junior high, my mom decided that my sisters and I needed to learn how to use money properly. My mom gave each of us a clothing allowance for the entire year in one lump sum.

My sisters blew through that money fast. They had a lot of clothing needs. But I didn't buy anything. My clothes were ratty and had holes in the knees and elbows. My mom got furious and lectured me.

But I didn't want to spend my money. Saving was far more compelling to me. That saving-at-all-costs approach lasted until I got married and had someone who understood spending better. Then, I finally understood I needed to make improvements.

I didn't understand how formative my parents' lessons on using money properly were at the time. Looking back, those simple lessons served me incredibly well. Knowing the basic elements of money proved to be a huge advantage.

So let's start with the fundamentals and build up from there. This will ensure everyone's on the same page.

Money Is a Tool

First, you must understand that money is just a tool.

Money is a tool in the same way a hammer is a tool. The hammer is simply a hammer. It has no feelings or thoughts about what you do with it. It doesn't know you. It doesn't conspire against you. Yet, people get incredibly emotional with money. They project a lot onto it.

So, step one, drop all the emotional baggage you've attached to money—it's just a tool.

Simply put, money is stored goods and services. It's potential energy waiting to be released. It also has power because it's your decision when and how it gets released.

Money also represents the exchange of goods and services. It's a huge improvement from thousands of years ago when bartering was how value was transferred from, say, a farmer to a builder: If you give me a few chickens, in exchange I will build something for you.

The collective idea of money grew out of those experiences. It went from a direct trade of goods and services into exchanging rocks, gold, silver, and salt. These symbols were easier to transport and reach agreements with.

Just like with any tool, money has a learning curve. If you practice diligently over time, you can master the tool. As a kid, you could bang a hammer to make a birdhouse. But if you stay with it, you can get to the point where you can build fine cabinetry or even a real house. It's the same with money. With enough practice, you can master money.

What You Can Do with Money

There are four things you can do with this tool: save it, spend it, invest it, and give it away. Each of these approaches to money requires you to grow. Think about each of these as part of your personal growth and development.

#1—Saving

Saving requires a future. If we were all going to die tomorrow, saving would be ridiculous. Since you likely will not, saving is essential.

In the future, there are certain needs that will recur (like groceries) and certain new needs will lie ahead (like having a first child or retiring from work).

If you're going to have a child, you may need a baby's room, a crib, and another car. You may also want to save for the child's college education. All these things start to roll out as a byproduct of thinking about the future. Therefore, saving requires hope, vision, discipline (over instant gratification), patience, and time. It requires a willingness to suffer a little now to create something bigger and better in the future.

Saving is empowering. When you know you can make things happen in your future, independent of anyone else, that's empowering and builds self-confidence.

I'd describe saving as delayed spending and giving. It buys you time to make clear, conscious choices about what the best use of those funds are for spending, giving, and investing. You're holding on to the funds in order to make the opportunity cost decision in the future.

In investing, there might not be any stocks I want to own right now, so I'm going to wait to invest. I'm going to sit on it until the opportunity comes.

It keeps your options open.

Perhaps you've already made the choice and value next fall's tuition over ice cream today. So you save money to be able to pay tuition.

This helps you step back from the trap of always spending what you make if you're geared that way. It's natural for us to be consumers. If you're always making short-term decisions, then you'll never build a long-term foundation. You'll never become empowered.

The delay mechanism is important. You could spend it later, but you're not going to spend it yet. It buys time to take a more thoughtful approach.

#2—Investing

Investing is a subset of saving. A portion of those savings dollars may be for goals that are several years or more away. With those dollars, you can consider the wider world of investment possibilities in search of higher long-term returns on your money. (I'll go into this a bit more in the Timeframes section.)

The primary area of investment this book will consider is stock investing. A stock is an ownership share in a corporation. When you buy a stock, you become part owner of that corporation. The stock market is a collection of publicly traded shares of corporations. I find it exciting to think that I can own part of a dynamic, growing corporation, even when I own just a few shares.

Other long-term investments that may be considered include bonds (bonds are issued when corporations borrow money—with a bond you become a lender to that corporation), real estate, and commodities.

#3—Spending

Spending is based on needs and wants. If you're oblivious to those, you'd never spend any money.

Spending comes in when you develop an egocentric view. There is a *you*, and this *you* needs to be fed. *You* want a new shirt and better shoes. *You* then choose to spend money on new shoes.

Our culture understands spending. My daughter understood spending at age three. She knew that if she wanted something, money could help her get it. That's the key understanding that most people still have of money.

#4—Giving

Giving is less understood.

Giving requires a larger world view, an awareness that others exist and have needs similar to your own. The act of giving develops one's capacity for compassion and empathy. While there are many ways to give, money can be used to help others get what they want and need.

It has been noted that among the universal human desires are to love, to be loved, and to make a difference in the world. These come together in the act of giving. It requires compassion for self and others. It requires awareness and maturity to understand that you can be a gift to others, and there is an appropriate time and place to offer that gift. As you give to the projects and people you most care about, you receive the satisfaction that comes with knowing you are making a difference. This giving includes your time, talent, and resources.

Giving can evolve to still higher levels. As you master the tool of money, you'll begin to see how taking an investment mindset to giving can geometrically expand its impact. This cast of mind can see the potential of ripple effects—the future returns on a given amount of capital. To see where a great idea is emerging and a tactical dose of capital could make all the difference. This sort of giving can be incredibly satisfying. The story of how this more advanced understanding around giving has unfolded for me is shared in Part Three. I hope it can be an inspiration for you in your journey.

Putting These Four Approaches into Practice

I recommend you do all of these (save, spend, invest, and give) in whatever measure works for you.

You'll learn more and more as you do this throughout your life. Your understanding will deepen in those different areas when you're ready.

I suggest starting by allocating 10% of your income to saving and 10% to giving. But, like in exercise and dieting, just getting started is key. Saving even 2% gets the wheel moving and allows you to start making progress.

OPPORTUNITY COST

Weighing things out logically takes emotion out of your decisions. It takes away the excitement from following the herd. A lot of the emotional troubles that plague people can be muted by using a clear, rational thought process.

Think in terms of opportunity costs. This means considering, "What is the best return I can get on each available dollar given all the competing opportunities for this dollar?"*

Looking at all the available options to determine the best return on your next dollar, you have four options:

- Saving the Dollar—Would it alter my future in an important way to save that dollar?

- Spending the Dollar—Would I gain significant personal satisfaction and value from having material things like a bigger TV or a better cellphone?

- Investing the Dollar—Could I make more than a dollar (i.e., $1.25) with this dollar?

- Giving the Dollar—What impact could it have on those people and causes I care about?

The Parking Meter

Let's look at an example of opportunity cost in action.

I routinely use parking meters even though I have a space in the parking garage next to my office. If I'm running from one meeting to another and I need to run into the office for a little while, I'll park out front at the meters.

---

* The corollary to opportunity cost is risk versus reward: "Where can I get the best reward with the least risk?"

The problem is that the best, most vigilant employee in our city is the meter maid. She must check our meters every five minutes.

Recently, I pulled up to a meter that had six minutes on it. I threw in a quarter for another 20 minutes. My next meeting was in 30 minutes, so I reasoned that I'd be back before the meter ran out. The right answer would have been to put another quarter in to be safe since a ticket would cost me $9 (36 times more than a quarter). But I didn't put in another quarter. The cheap part of me thought, "This will just work out. It'll be fine."

When I came out 28 minutes later, there was a ticket waiting for me. For $9, I got another two minutes of parking. That's expensive time.

It was a failure in my opportunity cost thinking:

1. What is the risk if I don't do this? $9

2. What is the risk if I do this? A quarter.

3. $9 is 36 times more than a quarter.

4. I chose to save the quarter.

5. I got a $9 ticket.

Even though that's a small decision, it has consequences. If I thought that way routinely, I would get to the end of the year and say, "I haven't saved much money." Maybe I'd say, "Life is hard. Things are expensive. I can't save." But the truth is that I just hadn't properly thought through my opportunity costs, day in day out.

Opportunity cost thinking is an incredibly useful tool for making all sorts of life decisions—especially in investing (as I will later show).

THE POWER OF COMPOUNDING

Albert Einstein said, "Compound interest is the eighth wonder of the world."

Compounding is a growth process where everything that grows is included in the next level of growth. Compound interest adds the principal (the initial amount) to the interest. Then interest grows on the new total amount, which is then added back to that amount. This cycle repeats over and over again.

Here's how it looks: The principal is $1,000. Let's say the interest rate is 5%, so the interest earned will be $50. Those are added together, so the principal is now $1,050. 5% interest on that would be $52.50. That's added back to the principal. It's now $1,102.50. And so on . . .

So each succeeding period, the total principal plus interest becomes a bigger number.

To illustrate the remarkable effects of how compounding small increments over time can truly matter, consider this:

Which would you rather have?

    A. $1,000 a day for the next 30 days

    B. Double the previous day's amount for 30 days starting with a penny

If you chose option A, you would collect $30,000. Not bad. But if you chose option B, you would collect $10.7 million.

You'll see how this extraordinary and disproportionate outcome occurs as we go.

Warning: Simple Math

I'm going to walk through this slowly so you can see how it builds.

This is simple math. The math I'll use is learned by the eighth grade. It's nothing fancy. It's just multiplication, division, addition, and subtraction.

Most people have the capacity to understand money and make it work for them with the math skills they've learned in our education system. It's just about applying those skills in an enlightened way.

Arithmetic Progressions

Compounding happens through progressions.

Let's begin with the progression people are most familiar with (whether or not they realize it): arithmetic.

Here's an arithmetic progression:

The Progression	The Math Behind It
1	1
2	1 + 1 = 2
3	2 + 1 = 3
4	3 + 1 = 4
5	4 + 1 = 5
6	5 + 1 = 6
7	6 + 1 = 7
8	7 + 1 = 8
9	8 + 1 = 9
10	9 + 1 = 10

What I want you to notice in the table is that I've gone from 1 to 10 in ten steps. This is an arithmetic progression we're taught at an early stage. It's called counting. As children, we can use our fingers and toes to do this. There's a strong focus on arithmetic progressions in our culture.

Geometric Progression

A geometric progression doubles the amount for each step.

The Progression	The Math Behind It
1	1
2	$1 \times 2 = 2$
4	$2 \times 2 = 4$
8	$4 \times 2 = 8$
16	$8 \times 2 = 16$
32	$16 \times 2 = 32$
64	$32 \times 2 = 64$
128	$64 \times 2 = 128$
256	$128 \times 2 = 256$
512	$256 \times 2 = 512$

In arithmetic progressions, the *amount* of increase is stable (adding one each time), but the *percentage* of increase declines over time. Often, that gets missed, and people don't think about it.

With geometric progressions, the amount of increase doubles each time while the percentage increase remains stable over time.

Arithmetic	% Increase	Geometric	% Increase
1		1	
2	100%	2	100%
3	50%	4	100%
4	33%	8	100%
5	25%	16	100%
6	20%	32	100%
7	16%	64	100%
8	14%	128	100%
9	12.5%	256	100%
10	11%	512	100%

Compare the two progressions. Notice the difference between the progressions at each step by looking at the third column.

Arithmetic	Geometric	Note that Geometric is:
1	1	Identical
2	2	Still identical
3	4	33% higher
4	8	2 times as much
5	16	3 times as much
6	32	5 times as much
7	64	9 times as much
8	128	16 times as much
9	256	28 times as much
10	512	50 times as much

Even though they started at the same point, after nine steps, the geometric progression has "earned" 50 times more than the arithmetic progression.

An arithmetic progression is what happened with my piggy bank. A geometric progression is what happens with compound interest. The leverage with compound interest is spectacular, but you don't see it until you get farther into the progression. The progression takes time to unfold.

The Rule of 72

Now let's look at how the power of geometric progressions applies to investing:

The Rule of 72

Rate of Interest × # of years = 72

The Rule of 72 is an equation that determines what it takes for your money to double.

It's an incredibly useful little trick. It's helpful for making quick calculations in your head. You just need to know the rate of interest and the time it takes.

Let's break it down with some examples.

If the rate of interest on your money is 6% and you had 12 years to leave it alone ($6 \times 12 = 72$), that's a double.

Let's say you want it to double in 10 years (___ $\times 10 = 72$). What rate would you need to earn? 7.2 %.

Let's say you want it to double in 5 years (___ $\times 5 = 72$). What rate would you need to earn? 14.4%.

Everyone could be a millionaire if they had enough time and an adequate rate of return.

If you had $1,000, how many doubles would you need to get to $1 million?

> 1 becomes 2, 4, 8, 16, 32, 64, 128, 256, 512, 1,024.

> 10 doubles on $1,000 gets you $1 million ($1.024 million, to be exact).

For simplicity's sake, let's say you could earn 7% a year. That's doubling about every 10 years (based on the Rule of 72 using 7.2% from above: $7.2\% \times 10 = 72$). Starting with $30,000, it would take 50 years to get 5 doubles and, thus, nearly become a millionaire ($960,000).

The geometric progress would look like this:

The Progression	The Math Behind It @ 7%
Year 1	$30,000
Year 10	$30,000 × 2 = $60,000
Year 20	$60,000 × 2 = $120,000
Year 30	$120,000 × 2 = $240,000
Year 40	$240,000 × 2 = $480,000
Year 50	$480,000 × 2 = $960,000

Start Early

With geometric compounding, it's not the doubling right now or the doubling in the next 10 or 20 years that makes the difference. It's the doubling you get 30 or more years out. That's why you should start saving as soon as possible. It's a slow accumulation of money at first, but after enough time has passed, the numbers suddenly get significantly bigger. Think about it: Whatever your last double was, that's half of all the money in the progression. The last double, then, is responsible for half of all your net worth.

Initial geometric compounding is boring. It's hard to see much difference. In the first step of either progression, one becomes two. You must have a long view. You won't experience the power until the second or third double. So the sooner you get started, the sooner you start enjoying the good part of the progression. You can then personally experience the extraordinary power of the eighth wonder of the world.

How Much Time Do You Have?

The problem with compounding is that it takes time. But time can be your greatest asset. Understanding timeframes cuts through a lot of confusion.

Our short-term, instant gratification society sensationalizes a lottery attitude. It discourages the responsible, though dull, savings orientation that makes people better off in the long run. For example, consider these two situations:

A. For the next 35 years, James spends $1 each day on a lottery ticket. Rounding down to $300 per year, over 35 years, James would spend $10,500 on tickets.*

B. For the next 35 years, Aaliyah invests $1 each day in a boring but consistent savings program (also rounding down to $300 per year).

In the first scenario, only a handful of the lottery tickets would win. Most lottery ticket buyers have little or nothing to show for their money.

In the second case, if the investment compounds at 7%, that person would have $44,374.

Timeframe with Stocks, Bonds, and Cash

Thinking in terms of timeframe is incredibly useful for deciding whether to invest in stocks.

According to the Ibbotson studies, if you go back to 1926, the stock market has had a 10% decline, on average, every other year. It's also had a 20% or larger decline every 3 to 5 years.

---

* The lifetime savings for the average American is $10,000.

The study also compared cash, bonds, and stocks over different segments of time during that same period. The researchers found, on average, the following is true:

- Over a 5-year period, stocks outperformed bonds and treasuries about 66% of the time.

- Over a 10-year period, stocks outperformed about 80% of the time.

- Over a 20-year period, stocks outperformed about 98% of the time.

The trend is clear. The more time you have, the more likely it is that stocks will outperform bonds and cash. Here's how to apply this information to your life:

- **If you need the money in the next 3–5 years (e.g., for a down payment on a house), leave it in the bank.** Your money should be in cash or cash equivalents so that when the money comes due, you'll have it—no questions asked. If it's in the stock market, it may be worth a lot less at the moment you need it.

- **If you don't need the money for 5 years or more, consider going with stocks.**

- **If your goal for the money is over 10 years away, (e.g., retirement or a college fund for a three-year-old), go with stocks.** The longer the timeframe you have, the more compelling stocks become.

You win in the long term, not the short term.

DON'T LOSE

N ow, let's combine our understanding of geometric progressions, opportunity costs, and timeframes to show how important it is to not lose money.

Warren Buffett, the world's greatest investor, is famous for saying, "Rule number one of investing is 'Don't Lose.' Rule number two? 'Read rule number one.'" This is why:

Compounding is the secret of a lifetime of wealth accumulation. Money lost cannot compound.

If you lose a dollar that could have compounded, what do you have? Nothing. It's gone. Money lost cannot compound. It's devastating.

You can double zero all you want, and it will never make a difference:

- Zero multiplied by zero is zero.

- Zero multiplied by ten is zero.

- Zero multiplied by a million is zero.

- Zero multiplied by anything is zero.

It's not that you just lost $1,000. You lost $1,000 *and* everything it could've created.

That changes the game, doesn't it? You should no longer take loss, especially foolish loss, lightly. So, don't lose.*

Regaining After a Loss

To further understand why not losing is so important, let's review losing investments. It takes far more to recover an investment loss than most people realize.

---

* I'll explain in more detail in future chapters.

For example, let's say you invest $100. Over the subsequent 3 years, it goes up 90%, down 70%, then back up 20%. How much do you have now?

The answer is counter-intuitive:

- $100 up 90% gives you $190.

- $190 down 70% leaves you with $57.

- $57 back up by 20% gives you $68.40.

So you would then need another *46% gain* on $68 to return to your original $100.

The math of losing money is perverse. *To offset a given percentage loss always requires one to earn a larger percentage gain.*

The Client Who Lost Big

I once met a woman who, at one point, had $220,000 in an IRA.* She then put the money in internet stocks during the dot-com bubble. After the bubble burst, she had only $20,000 left. It was a 90%+ loss.

When she came into my office, she told me she wanted me to turn the $20,000 back into $220,000. I told her, "I can do it, but you need a lot of time."

We then used the Rule of 72 to figure out how much time she needed. For $20,000 to go to $220,000, it would take between 3 to 4 doubles. At 10%, it would take about seven years per double. So, it would take about 24 years to regain her losses.

She was 40 when she first came in. She will be 64 and ready to retire when she finally recovers her loss.

Consider how much those two crazy years of bubble investing cost versus 24 years of sensible investing. Remember that every dollar is not just a dollar—it's all that it could become. If she hadn't lost the $220,000 and used it with that same 10% for those same 24 years, her account would have grown to $2.2 million. That's what she lost. She had the capacity to be a multimillionaire. But that capacity was destroyed with two years of frivolous investing.

---

* Individual retirement account

Locking in Losses

Knowing how damaging losing can be to the compounding process, let's look at the stock market.

In the stock market, if you sell during scary times, you'll "lock in losses." This fear-driven impulse is understandably human but, if acted upon, will prevent you from long-term growth.

Things will go wrong in the short run. The market can go up or down 20% at any time. It has many times already, and it will again. So it's essential to structure your financial portfolio in a way where you won't be forced to sell in a down market and, thus, avoid committing the mortal sin of locking in losses. There is no percentage gain that can offset that.

HOW TO HOLD ON TO YOUR MONEY

Now that you understand how important holding on to your money is, here are three strategies for handling your money well. They apply to everyone regardless of their position, wealth, or lack thereof.

#1—Spend Less Than You Make

In addition to saying, "Compound interest is the eighth wonder of the world," Albert Einstein also said, "He who understands it, earns it. He who doesn't, pays it."

Most people not only spend what they make, but they also borrow so they can spend even more. That's the power of compounding in reverse. If you're paying 12%–15% interest on a credit card or 10% on a car loan, you're compounding debt at an extraordinary rate.

While a house is an asset that can appreciate, all household goods depreciate. When you drive a car off the lot, it immediately declines in value. The same thing happens the minute you turn on a washing machine and use it. You cannot pay back the original loan with the asset you bought.

Later, you'll see that if you have debt (a mortgage, car loan, or student loan) and own stocks, you've borrowed to be in the stock market. When things go south, people with debt tend to get scared and liquidate their stocks, which, in turn, blows up their long-term game plan.

Being a saver and not a borrower has a huge impact over the span of a lifetime.

If your expenses are such that you cannot save, you need to make a change.

Let's say you live in San Francisco. If you make $50,000 a year and the rent is $3,000 a month ($36,000/yr), how do you live? Even at

$2,000 a month, that's $24,000/yr. That's half your income. That's too much.* The answer is, don't live in San Francisco. Maybe there are other factors that make it compelling to live there—but be aware if your expenses are more expensive than you can afford.

If you continually spend more than what you make, you'll never gain momentum.

Before the 1970s, spending more than you made was hard to do. Credit was hard to come by. Only a small percentage of the population had access to credit. You had to have collateral, standing in the community, or people to cosign for you to borrow money.

Then, in the 1970s, credit cards became much more accessible. Credit was democratized. Suddenly, anyone could be his or her own banker. It was remarkably freeing and exciting. However, for those who over-did it, it caused a lot of trouble.

Forty years later, that basic issue is still unresolved.

Now, the single largest category of indebtedness is student loan debt. Americans have a trillion dollars of student loan debt. It's horrible. Many 20- to 30- year-olds are so far behind the eight ball because of the massive debt they accrued during college. They often don't have the income to handle that debt, and it inhibits their ability to get into a winning game plan.

Credit, like money, is, in itself, not right or wrong, good or bad. But the abuse of credit has created problems.

So, spend less than what you make.

#2—Do a Monthly Budget

Make and follow a budget every month.

I recommend saving, giving, and investing before spending.

As human beings, we tend to spend whatever is in our pockets. I know this as well as anybody else. If I have $100 in my pocket, it's going out the door. If I put money in my wallet, it disappears over time. But if I've already done my saving, investing, and giving, I don't have to think about it. That is a great way to ensure you give and save.

As the often-quoted advice goes, "Pay yourself first." If the first dime goes into your savings or investment account, it's gone before you can spend it on anything else. If the next dime goes to giving, you can't spend that either.

---

* A good rule of thumb is that your housing cost should be no more than one-third of your income.

My advice is to spend 80% of what you make. Put aside 10% for giving and 10% for saving and investing, so you start to learn what those are about. If you structure your life in that way, you will learn much of what you need to know naturally.

We're wired for instant gratification and doing what feels good now. It's not wrong, but it's important to be aware of that. If you pay yourself first, you circumvent that. It's already done. Whatever you do with the rest of it, however idiotic it may be, you have your plan to keep you from failing. But if instead your plan is "I'll spend, then I'll save what remains," you're setting yourself up for failure.

Making a budget is about identifying priorities. After you save and give, do an opportunity cost analysis. Look at all the competing possibilities for your dollar. See where you get the best return.

While making a budget, if you're in debt, make it a priority to get out of debt.*

I recently did this analysis with a young friend of mine. He has four student loans at 4%, 3%, 2%, and 1.5%. If he's going to prepay some of his loans, it's clear that 4% is the one to pay off. That would give him the highest return on his dollar.

Then, let's factor in his 4% mortgage, which, since interest is deductible, actually costs him about 2.5% after taxes. His mortgage goes in the opportunity cost tree below his 4% and 3% student loans but above his 2% and 1% student loans.

He doesn't have credit card debt, but if he had credit cards at 10% or 15%, paying them off would be at the top. It's a good idea to pay off your credit card every month. I love the convenience of a credit card, but paying it off every month hugely minimizes the crippling effects of high interest.

#3—Keep an Emergency Fund

Emergencies are a part of life, so everyone should have a plan to handle them.

An emergency fund allows you to handle worse than average day-to-day luck. If your water heater goes out or your spouse backs the car into something, you can take it in stride financially because that's what the money is there for.

---

* This goes beyond the scope of this book. There are entire books and systems for getting out of debt. Many people have used Dave Ramsey's system to much success.

It ensures your long-term investments are uninterrupted by building a cushion between the short term and the long term. I've seen too many times where people have a short-term disaster (like a flooded basement), and then they have to liquidate their sound long-term investments to pay for the emergency. It blows their plan. So creating that cushion is crucial to being able to stay on course in the long term.

As a rule of thumb, have 6 months of living expenses in the bank (i.e., if your monthly expenses are $2,000, having $12,000 in savings is a good idea). If you have issues, like your employment is uncertain, it may be wise to make that emergency cash fund even larger.

This may not be possible, at least right away, so keep whatever is practical relative to your life situation.

Conclusion

If you're debt free, saving every month, and thinking long-term, these tools will help you sustain a long-term game plan. Your plan might fluctuate in value year to year, but it will prove lucrative in the long haul.

Choosing Your Path as an Investor

In the holy grail of value investing, *The Intelligent Investor*, Benjamin Graham wrote about the enterprising and the defensive investor:

> "The rate of return sought should be dependent on the amount of intelligent effort the investor is willing and able to bring to bear on this task. The minimum return goes to our passive investor, who wants both safety and freedom from concern. The maximum return would be realized by the alert and enterprising investor who exercises maximum intelligence and skill."

If you're an entrepreneurial investor,* you would say, "I want to be a business analyst. I want to study and own businesses. I want to find bargains and stocks that are cheap relative to their value, so I don't lose." (I'll dive into entrepreneurial investing in detail in the next chapter.)

If you don't want to spend a lot of time on investing in and analyzing businesses, you're a defensive investor. In that case, I encourage you to follow this outline:

- Maintain an emergency fund as a buffer so that you are never forced to sell (as I explained previously).

- Minimize taxes by funding all the retirement or tax-sheltered plans available to you, such as IRAs, 401(k)s, and so on.

- Invest in an S&P 500 index fund.

With discipline and planning, anyone can successfully follow this basic investing strategy.

---

* For our purposes, I'll call the Enterprising Investor the "Entrepreneurial Investor."

Minimize Taxes

As a defensive investor, use programs that encourage saving. The government wants you to save and has set up savings programs that offer you tax credits or tax breaks. Capitalize on those opportunities.

IRAs and Roth IRAs

Minimizing taxes is a key to compounding your wealth. IRAs and Roth IRAs are two great ways to go about that:

- **IRAs**—If your income is below a certain level, you can deduct contributions from your current taxes. Then, everything you earn in the account until you withdraw it compounds tax-deferred. Both the contributions and future earnings avoid current taxes. You are taxed only upon withdrawal.

- **Roth IRAs**—While the current contribution isn't tax deductible, everything you earn in the account compounds tax-free. At some future date when you take it out, ideally with a much larger sum, you pay no taxes.

Other Programs

- **401(k)**—If you work for a corporation, a 401(k) may be available. Take advantage of that, particularly if the corporation matches your contribution. If they match 3% of your income and you contribute up to 3%, that's a 100% return. You double that money overnight. You can't top that.

- **403(b) Plan**—If you work for a nonprofit, they may offer a 403(b) plan. It's essentially the 401(k) plan for nonprofits.

- **529 Plans**—There are 529 plans to help save for college. Most states will have a state tax deduction available up to a certain amount if you contribute to their 529 plan.

Keep It Simple and Know Your Opportunities

It's not like there's a hundred different things to consider. There's only a half dozen. Take the time to know which ones are available to you.

This will let you know how much of a benefit they are to you. That'll help you get more excited about it, too.

Learn the tax benefit of each option, and include it in your opportunity cost analysis.

Become knowledgeable about these programs so that you won't have to pay fees to an adviser year after year. There isn't a whole lot of change to these sorts of plans once you're set up.

Invest in an Index Fund

If you're a defensive investor, you're not looking to work too hard at investing. You want a long-term game plan that works. Luckily, index funds are available to you for just that.

The S&P 500 comprises 500 of the largest publicly traded companies in America. Investing in an S&P index fund is a sound way to own a piece of global capitalism. About 40% to 50% of the S&P's profits come from overseas. Even though the companies are U.S.-based, it has become a global marketplace.

You may see Coca-Cola as a U.S. company since it's based out of Atlanta, but 80% of the profits come from overseas. It's a U.S.-based entity, but it's a part of the global economy.

Today, the middle class in India is as large as the entire U.S. population. As incomes grow around the world, people like to eat better and buy higher-quality things, which will be good for business.

Remember that there will be volatility. Expect a 10% decline every 1 to 2 years, and a 20% decline every 3 to 5 years.

Use Dollar Cost Averaging

Commit a fixed amount of money to the market every month. When the market is high, you'll buy fewer shares because per share costs are higher. When the market drops, you'll buy a larger number of shares. You're automatically buying more at cheaper prices since per share costs are lower. It's a built-in way to have a lower than average cost relative to average price over the life of the asset.

These are the basics of the defensive investor. If you set these up, and stick to the long-term game plan, you'll do all right.

We've established the simple framework for what it would take to be a defensive investor. Why would you want to become a business analyst? It's a huge amount of time, cost, and effort to get great at that, after all. Why make the jump?

If you are predisposed to that sort of thinking and enjoy that process, you can outperform the defensive investor over time. You can get higher rates of return for yourself.

With this higher rate of return, you can more quickly reach your goals as an investor (remember the Rule of 72? A higher rate of return lessens the amount of time it takes to get to your goal).

I haven't put our clients' money in the S&P 500 index because, for example, using the entrepreneurial approach, we seek to do better for them with less risk over time.

If you want higher returns, invest the time and effort to master the skill set of the entrepreneurial investor. Part Two is for those who want to dig in and become business analysts. It's for those who probably found Part One a little too elementary.

LEVELS OF WEALTH BUILDING

Up to this point, building the blueprint to wealth has required you to call upon discipline, patience, and probably more math than you'd prefer. Now well-equipped, we can build upon this foundation with a logical framework that enables you to improve your financial future. I'll show you where all of this is headed and how your life can improve if you apply a logical approach to money.

There are four levels you can be in with money. If you follow this path, you can move through all the levels regardless of where you start.

Level One: Subsistence

Subsistence is where you're just trying to survive. You're making just enough to cover your primary needs (food, clothing, and shelter), but you have to scramble to do it.

Level Two: Building Empowerment

The building empowerment level is like the subsistence level, but you understand the importance of saving enough to do it anyway.

The woman with the handful of rice shows us that the scramble isn't necessarily about money. It's about understanding how the system works and how you can make optimal choices for yourself.

You make and follow a budget. You save, spend, invest, and give.

You have a savings account, and every month you put something away. You take full advantage of what's available to you as best you can. It takes discipline and sacrifice, but it gets you moving in the right direction.

In this step, you're going from one to two in your progression. Again, it may not seem like much, but you're on the path and making progress. That's significant.

Level Three: In the Swim

In this step, you've got structures in place. You've found your rhythm. You're now thinking 30 years out. You haven't made a million dollars yet, but it's starting to feel like a real possibility. It's becoming something that could happen.

You've seen your account balance grow and your money double a couple of times—$10,000 became $20,000, then $40,000. You've felt an increase in confidence. You're deepening your understanding of how this process works. You see a much bigger picture for your life.

Let's say you manage to accumulate your first $100,000. That's just 3.5 doubles away from $1,000,000. That's so close. At this point, you can see it. You can taste it. You know that it's going to work if you stay on the path. You're going to get there.

Being in the swim comes with a great surge of confidence. Instead of guessing, you have a better sense of how things work. You have personal experience of seeing the wealth-building process unfold (which is materially different from talking about it or reading it in a book).

It also gives you more room to handle failure. Now, even if you take a hit, you know how to get back in the game and not be derailed.

Be warned: You might be tempted to think that you're at the mountain top. If you started at subsistence level and then accumulated $100,000, you might feel you've arrived and want to cash out.

Don't make this mistake.

I've seen people who, after all this hard work and patience, just go through the money in a couple of years. It's a shame. It happens all too often.

Remember, you're on an upward path. It will only improve as you continue. Each double you do increases how much the next double will be. Half of all your wealth is waiting in the next double.

Your mindset starts shifting. You're rich in comparison to where you started, but you're not rich compared to where you're going to be. You're on new ground you've never seen before. You realize there's an even better land down the road.

Hold the line and keep going because then that sets you up for the next step—freedom.

Level Four: Freedom

When money gets to be sizable enough, it doubles into the millions. Everyone can be a millionaire. You just have to start soon enough and stay disciplined with your savings, minimize taxes, and earn a decent rate of return.

If you have $1,000,000 invested, earning 7% a year, you could withdrawal 5%, $50,000 (the national average income) a year to live on without working (or in addition to any income you make). And you can leave the principal and other 2% of earnings to keep compounding. This preserves the principal, which can continue to throw money off and grow indefinitely.

You are at a point of financial independence. Your assets are working for you. It's a material shift in possibilities. Most of our parents and grandparents worked their whole lives because they had to. But, at this level, working becomes voluntary. You can now choose to do work that provides little or no pay but has tremendous benefits to yourself and others.

Having this possibility is relatively new.

At the end of 2013, there were four million millionaires in America. That means 1.2% of the population can be at this freedom level if they control their expenses.* These millionaires have enough capital to expand their menu of choices in life. They can move or take a big trip or go back to school and get a higher degree. They can act with flexibility.

Consider how empowering "I know what I want to do, and I'm going to go do it" is versus "I know what I want to do, but I can't because I don't make enough money." A lot of people get stuck with the latter. But you don't have to.

Having a regular savings program enables many people to move from Subsistence to Building Empowerment, then to In the Swim then on to the Freedom level.

---

* The stories of professional athletes going broke, rather than being free, are largely due to not controlling expenses.

ACTION STEPS: PART ONE

Here is a distilled down version of all the actions you can now take now that you've read and understood what came before:

Remember, money is just a tool. Drop all the emotional baggage you've attached to it. Practice diligently and consistently, and you will master it.

Save, spend, invest, and give in whatever measure works for you. I suggest allocating 10% of your income to giving and 10% to saving. But as with exercise and dieting, just getting started is key.

Most people have the capacity to understand money and make it work for them with the math skills they have. Start applying those skills in an enlightened way.

The leverage with compound interest is spectacular, but it takes time to unfold. Take the long view and start saving as soon as possible. The sooner you get started, the sooner you start benefitting.

Forget the lottery attitude. Instead, take on a responsible, though dull, savings orientation that leaves you better off in the long run.

Think about the timeframe of your goals in order to decide whether to invest in stocks. If you need the money in the next 3–5 years, leave it in the bank. If you don't need the money for 5–10 years, consider stocks. If your goal is 10+ years away, go with stocks.

Compounding is the secret of a lifetime of wealth accumulation. But money lost cannot compound. So no longer take loss, especially foolish loss, lightly. Don't lose.

In the stock market, if you sell during scary times, you'll "lock in losses." This fear-driven impulse, if acted upon, will prevent you from long-term growth. So structure your financial portfolio in a way that you won't be forced to sell in a down market and, thus, you avoid committing the mortal sin of locking in losses.

Follow these three strategies to avoid that: 1) spend less than you make, 2) make and follow a monthly budget, and 3) keep an emergency fund.

Choose your path as an investor: defensive or entrepreneurial.

If you're a defensive investor, research and set up programs that minimize taxes. Invest in an index fund and use dollar cost averaging to commit a fixed amount of money to the market every month.

If you're an entrepreneurial investor, invest the time and effort to master the skill set. Read Part Two to dig in and start learning how to be a business analyst.

Regardless of which path you choose, you can start, or continue to climb, the four levels of wealth.

Even if you are at the Subsistence level and are struggling, start saving anyway. Make and follow a budget. Save, spend, invest, and give in whatever measure works for you. Have a savings account, and put something away every month. Take full advantage of what's available to you as best you can. Be disciplined. Sacrifice.

When you've got structures in place and are now thinking 30 years out, stay on the path. You're going to get there. You might be tempted to think that you're at the mountain top. You might feel you've arrived and want to cash out. But hold the line, and keep going because then that sets you up for the next step, which is freedom.

When money gets to be sizable enough, it doubles into the millions. With $1,000,000 invested, earning 7% a year, you could withdraw 5% a year to live on ($50,000, the national average income), and leave the remaining principal and 2% of earnings to keep compounding and growing indefinitely.

PART 2

MAXIMIZING RETURNS: THINKING LIKE AN ENTREPRENEURIAL INVESTOR

As I said previously, if you want higher returns from your investments, invest the time and effort to master the skill set of the entrepreneurial investor. Part Two is for those who want to dig in and become business analysts. It's for those who probably found Part One a little too elementary.

For Part Two, I'm going to start treating you more like you have some investment experience. I won't try to give you exhaustive detail for every concept, but instead try to give you a fuller picture of the investing landscape. There will be fewer specifics and more broad strokes about how to think about your investments, how to set up an effective investment program, and how to structure your affairs.

Part Two aims to give you an idea of what you need to know and how those factors interact with each other. A lot of the underlying details will go beyond the scope of this book. But in the age of the internet, there are many ways to fill in the gaps with detailed information.

This wider picture will inform your future development and create a strong framework to work within.

If you get overwhelmed in the entrepreneurial investor section, skip ahead to Part Three.

DEVELOPING CLEAR THINKING

Clear, logical, and unemotional thinking is at the heart of any great entrepreneurial investor. So let's take a step back and think about thinking.

As an entrepreneurial investor, you are involved in inquiry and investigation. If you're going to investigate, you need a solid thinking framework so that you stay on track and don't get pulled aside by those who are manipulative or unintentionally misleading. You need to be clear about what's true and what you most need to know.

The best and clearest thinking process I've ever come across is in *Filters Against Folly* by Garrett Hardin. In his analysis, there are three filters that you should use to refine and improve your thinking:

1. The Literate Filter

2. The Numerate Filter

3. The Ecolate Filter

The Literate Filter

The literate filter asks, "What are the words?"

Hardin asserts that our society is primarily literate. We're biased toward literacy. Of the three R's (reading, writing, and arithmetic), two of them are literate (reading and writing).

But words can obscure and confuse as often as they illuminate (if not even more often). If you're not alert to how words are used, you can be easily fooled.

The choice of language has a psychological effect and can influence others.

He asserts that the pharmaceutical industry created the term "side effects" to minimize concern about the consequences of taking a drug.

When we hear "side effects," we tend to drop our guard. We may think, "Oh, that's unlikely," or "That won't hurt too much." Our focus turns to the drug's stated benefit, and we discount the negatives. According to Hardin, there are only *effects*. There's no such thing as side effects.

As another example, the term "revenue enhancement," a favorite of politicians, is just a nicer term for a fee or tax increase.

As a third example, at one point in the 1990s, the so-called dot-com boom got so bad that if a company was a dot-com company, people automatically wanted to buy it. They had no idea what it did, what its business plan was, or whether it had any revenue. But if it was a dot-com company, people had to own it.

During that period, a man called me and said he wanted a hundred shares. I asked, "A hundred shares of what?" He said, "Dot-com." I asked, "Well, which company?" He didn't know. He didn't care. He just wanted a hundred shares of "dot-com." If it had "dot-com," that's what he wanted. He didn't need to know anything else.

As human beings, words matter. In our culture, we routinely get fooled by them. So, to protect yourself, use the literate filter. Ask, "What are the words being used? What is the real message being conveyed?"

The Numerate Filter

For much of our literate society, the idea that the internet was going to change the world was exciting. Therefore, investing in stocks with dot-com in the name made sense. But if the numbers don't add up, regardless of how eloquently named it may be, it should be avoided. This is where the numerate filter comes in. It asks, "What are the numbers?"

Hardin states that our culture is innumerate (i.e., illiterate with numbers). We don't understand math well. We don't apply math well.

Once again, investing doesn't require complex math. A few concepts carry most of the freight.

Yet, people are routinely fooled by numbers. They can't make sense of money coming in, money going out, and how those two match up.

In the previous chapter, I mentioned how bad consumer debt has become. Student loans alone are a trillion dollars. How did that happen?

A common accusation is that the lenders and universities are predatory. However, students aren't children, either. They presumably learned high school math, but they are failing to apply it. Students, when enrolling in college, don't have a sense of, "I'm borrowing this much money, here's how much I am likely to make, this is how much my expenses will be, and it will cost this much to pay it back (the principal plus interest)."

Knowing the numbers and making an intelligent choice based off the numbers is largely lacking.

As we get into the investment realm, you'll find out that numeracy is paramount. It's the essence of entrepreneurial investing:

- What are the numbers?

- What is the business worth?

- What is the price?

  - If the worth is higher than the price, it's a bargain, and I'll consider buying it.

  - If I own it and its worth is dramatically less than the price, then I'll sell because I'll get more than it's worth.

How could you invest any other way? Yet, people do it all the time. They often don't even ask what the numbers are. They just see products and think, "It's cool. Everyone likes it. I think I'll buy into that company."

The Ecolate Filter

The ecolate filter asks, "And then what?"

Ecolate derives its name from ecology. Ecology is the study of the natural environment and all its interconnected factors. It thinks in terms of systems not components.

Hardin argues that everything is connected. Everything has a ripple effect. You have to take a bigger view when you make decisions. You have to see the world as a system where all factors are related. You cannot change just one thing.

He goes through numerous policy changes at governmental levels and the unintended consequences that can spool out.

In 1985, Hardin described how the U.S. Army Corp of Engineers built levees up and down the Missouri River in order to protect cities and assets from floods. The unintended effect was that the levees channeled the river and made it run faster and higher. As the silt deposits at the river's bottom rose, floods likely would be far bigger than average. Normal buffers like marshes and water running over the banks were taken away. So, in essence, Hardin argued that the U.S. Army Corp of Engineers unwittingly maximized the potential damage of a flood.

Hardin was right. In 2011, an area of South Dakota had a major flood where an entire community had to be evacuated.

In the investing world, as people start to pay more attention to a certain area, funds start moving in that direction. If a tech fund manager is sent money to buy more tech stocks, that's what he has to do. That's what he is paid to do—whether or not it makes sense to buy at that price. If enough people demand it, this forced buying makes the stocks go up. The rising stock price makes people more excited. They tell everyone the "good news." They and their buddies buy more of the stocks. Prices are starting to spiral up.

At some point, prices become completely out of proportion to underlying value, and there's now no one new left to buy. The next major move will be down. People start selling. The price plummets. If you were that excited about it, you're probably not going to get out right away. It will probably be down 30% before you start thinking, "Maybe I shouldn't have done this."

When the dot-com bubble burst, it went down 90%.

To avoid being stuck in a crashing market, you need to take a bigger view of the entire system as you make decisions.

Using the Filters in Investing

These filters are simple but powerful. At first, they may seem clunky and cumbersome. As you consistently apply them, though, they become integrated in your thinking. You'll start to do it naturally.

Eventually, you may find you cannot read the front page of the paper without applying all three filters. Every story you read can be analyzed in this way. You can find all kinds of gaping flaws in people's logic and see their poor choices as a result.

These tools can and should be used when you're reading a report, the *Wall Street Journal,* and your news feed on the internet. If you do, you'll see how loose the thinking is out in the world. Most people lack a rigorous thought process.

To be a successful entrepreneurial investor, you'll need to rise above all that and see things clearly.

BECOMING A BUSINESS ANALYST

Ownership: An Introduction

Every year since 1982, *Forbes* has published a list of the 400 wealthiest Americans. In recent years, it expanded the list to the 400 wealthiest people in the world.

Where did this wealth come from? How did these individuals get so wealthy?

Virtually all of the 400 wealthiest people are business owners: Microsoft's Bill Gates, Telefonos de Mexico's Carlo Slim, Walmart's the Waltons, Berkshire Hathaway's Warren Buffett, Amazon's Jeff Bezos . . . the list goes on and on.

Wealth in this world is created through business ownership. If you want to increase your rate of wealth-building, you need to own businesses.

Stocks are one way to gain ownership in a business. You can buy shares in a publicly traded company and participate in the increase in wealth created by that business over time. If the company's leader is thinking long-term and has a mission to grow the value of the enterprise, you get to tag along as a shareholder.

Now that you're going to own businesses (via stocks), the logical question is, "Which businesses do you want to own?"

As an entrepreneurial investor, you must be able to analyze the following aspects:

- What makes a good company?

- Which variables are most important?

- What is it worth (value)?

- What is the cost (price)?

- Is this something worth buying after you compare the price and the value?

For me, this process is highly engaging and fun to do. It's bargain hunting. I love being on the lookout for treasures.

Price and Value

Price is what you pay. Value is what you get. As simple as it sounds, the majority of the investment world seems disinclined to this view.

How do you distinguish between the price and the value of a company?

1. Before you look at the price, determine what the business is worth (within a range).

2. Look at the price, and then ask a few key questions:

   A. Does the price reflect that value?

   B. Is this price substantially more than the value?

   C. Is this price substantially less than the value?

Do the math. Forget the market while you do your analysis. If you already own it, ask yourself, "If I didn't own it right now, would I buy it?" Your assessment will tell you whether to buy, sell, hold, or pass.

- If the price is reasonable, hold it.

- If the price is significantly higher than what you came up with, sell it or pass.

- If the price is significantly lower, hold it or buy it.

That's always the process. It's simple, but its value comes in applying it.

Make your own judgments. If you don't, then you're lost. You're subject to the illogical and counter-productive whims of the market.

ACCOUNTING: THE LANGUAGE OF BUSINESS

A key area to understand is accounting. Accounting is the language of business. If you're going to be an entrepreneurial investor, you must learn how to read a balance sheet and an income statement. It's not rocket science, but it's not self-evident, either. You need to spend time on accounting to gain a basic understanding.

Accounting has a lot of facets. It goes beyond the scope of this book. I recommend the book *The Interpretation of Financial Statements* by Benjamin Graham and Charles McGoldrick.

To get you started, however, here are some brief descriptions of key terms you will want to know and pay attention to:

Financial Statement

A financial statement is a snapshot of how things are going. It is intended to give an accurate picture, an accounting, of a company's condition and operating results in a condensed form. By comparing a current financial statement to past financial statements, you can build a picture of how the company is evolving over time. This, in turn, equips you to better gauge the value of the business and future possibilities for the company and its stock price. The financial statement contains two major parts: an income statement and a balance sheet.

Income Statement

The income statement shows how much money ("net income" or "earnings") the company made for the reporting period. Essentially, net income is the cash the company has left over after deducting all costs and expenses from total sales. While it sounds simple, you will want to know how the income is calculated. Companies have various ways to calculate each of the items that go into the net income. Aggressive managers often use aggressive accounting measures. Conservative managers often use conservative accounting measures. Understood this way, accounting and how the numbers are prepared offers a window into the style and intentions of the managers.

Balance Sheet

A balance sheet is a listing of what the company owns and owes. The balance sheet gives a sense of the company's strength. In particular, pay close attention to how much the company owes. When times get tough, companies that owe a lot generally have the most difficulties. More debt usually means more risk.

Ratios

As important as knowing what the numbers are, it's even more important to know what the numbers mean. It's the relationship of those numbers that provide the meaning. That's where ratios come in.

As a value investor, you're a bargain hunter. To know if a company is selling at a bargain price, it helps to have some ratios of valuation in your back pocket. Some ratios you will want to learn include the price/earnings (PE) ratio, the price/sales ratio, and the price/book value ratio. Each of these can improve your sense of whether a company's stock price is especially cheap or expensive at a given point.

Scale

Scale is a ratio of relative size. Scale puts numbers into perspective. For example, how scared should investors be about economic problems in Greece? Answer: Not very. Greece represents just 0.2% of the global economy. Yet, because they lack an understanding of scale, economic issues in Greece have caused many investors much hand-wringing. To get perspective, then, understand scale.

Interest Rates

The single most important factor in the valuation of assets is the level of interest rates. In general, declining interest rates lead to higher asset valuations. Rising interest rates lead to declining asset valuations. This is huge, yet far too little understood by most investors. Take time to understand the relationship of changes in interest rates to asset prices.

Return on Equity and Profit Margins

Return on equity and profit margins are measurements of how efficiently a company is being run. Equity is capital used to run the business. Return on equity, then, tells us how much earnings we can expect the company to produce from a given dollar of capital. Profit margins tell us how much of each dollar of sales becomes net income. Compared with the profit margins of competitors, this number can tell us a lot about how well the operations are run.

Capital Allocation

As money rolls into a business, what does it do with the cash? That's capital allocation. How management decides to allocate each extra dollar that comes in highly impacts the long-term development of business value.

Summary

Accounting is the language of business. If you're going to be an entrepreneurial investor in search of maximizing your returns, accounting proficiency is essential. Take the time to become fluent in accounting.

What It Takes to Grow

Consider how much capital the business requires to grow. Capital is the resources devoted to creating goods and services. Resources include money, raw materials, factories, trucks, and so on.

Companies that require little capital are attractive to me. I love businesses that require small amounts of capital in order to grow. It means there'll be much more profit for you to pocket.

If I run a railroad in a highly inflationary world, the cost of capital is high and rising. Steel costs go up. The cost of building more track goes up. It's expensive to lay each mile of railroad in order to create more income and profit. The railroad business is capital intensive.

On the other hand, if I am an online publisher that sells subscriptions for $100 a year to my publication, the incremental cost for 100 more people to buy it is almost zero. That next $10,000 of subscription revenue is essentially all profit.

Accounting Shenanigans

Coca-Cola owns bottlers all over the world. In the 1990s, when the company was running a little short of its projected numbers, it would sell a bottler in order to record a big profit and make or beat its projected number. Everyone would say, "Oh, you've beat the numbers again. You guys are amazing."

But there's a substantial difference between an operating profit and selling assets to raise cash. Selling assets often diminishes future earning power. It's a short-term strategy that can backfire in the long run.

Capital Allocation

To better understand capital allocation, let's look at a child's lemonade stand. Susie purchases the materials she needs—lemons, sugar, ice, pitchers, and glasses. She does some marketing by hanging her sign on her card table and posting signs on nearby telephone poles. She's a savvy businessperson. She's focused on the variables of her business.

After some success, she now has to determine the best way to spend each dollar of profit to develop and grow her business. With a better quality product, she may get more customers. She could also expand her business to a second location. She could buy another card table and put up another lemonade stand. Optimizing this decision is what capital allocation is all about.

Now let's go back to the world of publicly traded companies.

At some point in every successful business, capital allocation becomes as important as —or more important than—the business operation. What the business does with its cash will highly impact the long-term value of the business.

There are five things a publicly traded company can do with that extra dollar:

1. Grow the business.

2. Acquire other businesses or assets.

3. Pay down debt (if you have debt).

4. Pay a dividend and give some of that cash back to your shareholders.

5. Buy back stock.

This is another opportunity cost decision.

When I got involved in investing in the 1980s, Buffett was virtually alone in talking about buybacks and capital allocation. He said that it's as if you trained your whole life to play the violin, and when you finally get to Carnegie Hall, they ask you to play the piano. That's exactly how it is with most of corporate America.

What happens often in corporate America is that the CEO is the person who figured out how to source the lemons and save the company a bunch of money. She was great at operations. But as CEO, she isn't being asked to source lemons anymore. She's being asked how to allocate funds. She has no training for the most important decisions she needs to make.

HUNTING FOR TALENT

In any field, there are people who are markedly better than the rest. That's part of what's so exciting about watching the Olympics. The athletes perform at a high level and excel under pressure.

The same level of talent exists in business. Some people are just wired for it. They've been working at it from an early age. They're curious and open to learning, so they've accumulated lots of wisdom. They have a unique skill set. They network well.

You can take your investing up another level by restricting your investments to the very best people, such as Warren Buffett. Our largest holding with our clients, for a long time, has been Buffett's company, Berkshire Hathaway. That has proven incredibly valuable for us.

It is worth paying attention to those companies that are exceptionally well run. It can be valuable to read their reports and attend their meetings to see how some of the best and brightest think about business.

You can find them by looking at their track records.

One of my father's favorite maxims was, "What gets measured gets done." As a shareholder, it's a good habit to monitor the companies you own to see if they do what they say they'll do.

It's a rare CEO who . . .

- has a vision.

- is honest about what he or she says.

- sets clear goals.

- holds himself or herself accountable to achieving those goals.

- has a high and rising level of performance in the business over time.

Most companies put up a target and do one of the following:

- If they hit the target, they'll tell you all about it. Hitting that target could be a function of excellent execution, or it could just be a function of luck. Either way, they'll take credit.

- If they don't hit the target, they will change targets and say, "We've reviewed our long-term goals, and we're going to go in a new direction." Then, they set up new targets they may or may not hit.

Great companies are clear about which metrics matter and hold themselves to that standard. That creates a culture that is clear about what needs to happen. What gets measured is what gets done.

Corey, my partner at Pecaut & Company, keeps a whole file of what he calls "*Except For* Companies." Year after year, such companies would've hit their goals *except for* some unexpected event. In reality, they're just making excuses.

Typically, such companies suggest that they are victims of circumstances rather than empowered organizations that do what they set out to do, in spite of the occasional setback.

It's uncommon to think instead that "We're going to set a goal where we can take a few hits, a few unexpected turns, and still make it. We expect to make it in spite of a few setbacks." What happens more often is the numbers say one thing and the words say another.

By watching how people and businesses behave over time, you won't have to be surprised by what may happen.

If people have a track record of being shady, cutting corners, and making excuses, when things get tough, you can expect they'll do more of the same.

If people have a record of integrity, they under-promise and over-deliver, and they think clearly about difficult positions, you can expect that they'll perform reasonably well when things get tough.

THE OWNERSHIP
SHORTCUT

One way to bypass many of the variables involved with picking a stock is to focus on ownership.

I'm amazed at how little discussion is given to this basic fact on Wall Street. Ownership is seldom mentioned in reports.

I want to know who owns the company. If its managers don't own it, why should I? I want to invest in businesses where the people running it are up to their eyeballs in that business, and their family net worth is on the line. This doesn't guarantee success, but it minimizes what can go wrong.

The reason is, ownership drives stewardship. When I was younger, I did a lot of public speaking. During speeches, I would ask the audience a series of questions:

> "How many of you have ever rented a car?"
>
> *[All the hands would go up.]*
>
> "And how many of you have ever washed a rental car?"
>
> *[All the hands would go down.]*
>
> "Well, if the car's dirty, why wouldn't you wash it?"
>
> Invariably, somebody would say, "Well, it's not my car."
>
> "Exactly. That's my point. The same applies to business."

All of us have an acute sense of *what's mine* vs. *what's not mine*. If it's my car, it's my job to wash it. If it's not my car, it's somebody else's job to wash it. So, at a fundamental level, it's a psychological shift to say, "I own this. This is mine."

I've learned, over time, that many businesses are run in a less than professional manner. Board members often act in their own self-interests or political interests—not in the economic interests of the shareholders. That's better known now. But people don't realize how widespread it is, particularly in smaller companies.

I learned this the hard way through my experience with American Guaranty.

No Skin in the Game

American Guaranty sold burial insurance (which is a profitable business to be in). Its stock sold about 20% below what its assets were worth. It made sense to my numeric filter.

Then, American Guaranty's management had a crazy idea. They decided to build a coal pier in Portland and ship coal to Asia. So, they invested the conservative reserves of the insurance company into this risky endeavor. It wasn't conservative. It was speculative and capital-intensive.

When I heard about their plan, I got nervous. Then, in a subsequent earnings release, the company had some questionable write-offs. This gave me a sinking feeling in my stomach. Something was wrong.

So my father and I flew out to Oregon to check it out. I was stunned by what I saw. The CEO not only didn't seem to know what was going on within the insurance company, but his next investment idea was to buy sticker kiosks in malls because "kids love stickers." I was astounded by his lack of business focus. There was no numeracy. There was no discussion of "this many kiosks should generate this much revenue and get this much return." It was just, "Kids like 'em." It was horrifying. There were red flags everywhere.

Shortly after my visit, Leucadia National bought the burial insurance business from American Guaranty. It bought American Guaranty's golden goose and didn't even pay above book. American Guaranty gave it away because it wanted capital to do these oddball things.

So, I called all my clients and told them, "We're down on the investment about 30%. We need to get out of here." Some clients were upset, but it had to happen based on this new information.

Afterward, I did a postmortem. I realized that the insiders owned only 3% of the company. Nobody had significant skin in the game. It was like a plaything to them.

That was such a valuable learning experience for me. I said to myself, "Dan, you need to know who owns these things, not just what their thinking process is. If management doesn't own it, then you need to be super careful."

Over the years, I've seen this rule proven. Duro-Test and Safeguard Business Systems are two more examples. Management didn't own a lot of stock. They both sold out at low prices. In both cases, it looked like their goal was job security. They figured, "Well, if we can get bought out by the right people and keep our jobs, that's in our best interest."

You may think it's surprising that the shareholders let it happen, but this happens all the time in smaller businesses that aren't institutionally owned. The ownership base is diffused among small investors who don't have the resources, or the will, to challenge such decisions.

My main piece of advice when looking at companies, then, is to always ask the question: Who owns it?

There's an old saying: "I want them to eat their own cooking." If the management of the company own a substantial portion (say 20% or more, or enough where their families' respective net worth is on the line), that doesn't mean they won't be stupid or dishonest. But it does substantially mitigate some of those risks because they'll lose more than you will if things go bad. At its best, it creates companies where people think long-term. They make opportunity cost and risk-reward decisions with long-term views. Those can be outstanding companies to invest in.

If a business has strong owner/management and a public price, a lot of intensity can go into creating a strong public track record. The owner's thinking is probably, "I want this to do well. When I look back on my life's work, I want this to be something I can be proud of." That ownership-driven attitude is rare. But that's the type of company I want.

If the people running the company are intelligent owners, they're always thinking about the long-term good. However, many large corporations are not run that way.

The Hired Hand Mentality

In most large corporations, the CEO is a hired hand who is paid well. He wants to be a star during his tenure. That promotes short-term decision-making. The CEO may do things to expand his empire so that he makes more money for himself, but these choices rarely serve the shareholders in the long term. All too often with hired hands, more is detracted from value than added.

So own companies where the owners are running the show. Berkshire Hathaway is the ultimate example of this.

I remember Charlie Munger, now Buffett's partner at Berkshire Hathaway, talking at a Wesco meeting in the late 1980s about the danger of hired hands. At the time, the savings and loan industry was heading into a crisis. Munger saw it, but most of the world didn't.

Munger pointed out that if you have a hired hand making large decisions about loans, the worst outcome for the hired hand is losing their job. But the system's worst outcome is that the bank goes down and chaos ensues. The hired hand doesn't have enough of a personal stake in the game to make the more intelligent decision to decline the loan.

That's what happened with Chuck Prince, the CEO of Citigroup, in July 2007. He was at the top of the whole subprime mortgage boom. He said this, "As long as the music is playing, you need to get up and dance. We're still dancing." So, here's the head of one of the largest banks in the world effectively saying, "I know this is wrong. I know this will end badly. But I have to do this because everyone else is doing it."

I understand the pressure on him. If he had said no when it was the responsible thing to say (several years prior), he would have been dismissed as CEO. The board would have said, "If you're not going to play, we'll get someone who will. We've got to out-compete the other banks. If we say no, everyone else will get all that business."

Prince was a hired hand. If the company had been Chuck Prince Savings and Loan Bank, with the Prince family name going back five generations, would he have made those loans? Clearly, he would have been more careful.

That's the difference of ownership versus hired hands. It's hardly ever mentioned in the reports I read.

Though I didn't immediately realize it, one of the things that has helped me enormously as an investor was running my business. Being a business owner gave me a gut understanding of human resources, dealing with staff, regulations, licensing, dealing with the government, paying taxes, the effects of technology, systems, structures, competition, and marketing. All of these things exist in any business, even a small one like ours.

The Crux of Why Ownership Matters

Having our own business makes us alert to how much time and money can get squandered or focused on different priorities, such as politics, friendly relations, owing people favors, or tradition ("This is the way we've always done it"). I respect loyalty and the fact that their great-grandfather founded the company and ran things a certain way. But if the world shifts and there's a better way to do things, that's what you should do.

When my partner and I go into corporate boardrooms and talk to chief financial officers (CFOs), we can ask detailed questions and pick up on things that don't fit. That's what happened at Landmark Graphics.

Landmark Graphics did software for the oil service industry. I'm not a tech guy, so I couldn't gauge whether the software was the best or if competition could take its business away. But the oil services area had been depressed for a while. We like industries that have had huge declines. People lose a lot of money, get angry, and their attitude becomes, "I'll never buy that stuff again." That's a great setup for a value investor.

Landmark was in that bucket. Its share prices dropped from $30 per share to $15–$20 per share. It had no debt. It generated cash. It had high returns on capital like a lot of software companies. We decided to check it out and flew to Houston to meet with its management.

The first thing we noticed was the beauty of the Landmark office. It had a huge atrium with palm trees. There were basketball and tennis courts. Clearly, Landmark Graphics was being run for employees with the philosophy of "Let's make everyone happy," which isn't wrong. But that may be different from what's in the best interest of shareholders.

After exchanging some pleasantries, the CEO answered some of our questions about the business. Then the CFO started bragging about the company's recent real estate purchase. Corey, my partner, then asked a devastating question, "Well, are you in the real estate business or the software business?"

The CFO did not like that. A dark cloud moved into the room. I asked, "Why aren't you buying back your stock when it is so cheap?" When prodded, he had no intelligent answer regarding their capital allocation plans. The CFO just told us the company wasn't going to do that.

We left feeling that Landmark Graphics was not interested in the shareholders. Yet, it was an interesting business. It was a leader in its field. It had no debt and generated a lot of cash. We decided we would buy the stock only at around $16 per share. Then, we would risk management blowing money on employees and hope for outside catalysts to create value. That's exactly what happened. A couple years later, Halliburton bought it out at $30 per share.

Phantom Ownership

That said, not all ownership is good ownership. There are three kinds of phantom ownership to avoid: stock options, large industries, and family ownership (in name only).

In the 1990s, using stock options as compensation for employees ramped up. Stock options work with this implicit agreement:

"I'm not putting any money in. But the company gives me the right to buy the stock at a certain price. I don't have any risk. If the stock goes south, my options didn't cost anything. But if it goes up, I can use the cash from the conversion to pay for the exercise. It's like a giant bonus."

So the psychological makeup of the stock option holder is significantly different from owners who have put up their own money and have skin in the game.

It's in the interest of the option holder to see the stock price as high as possible at the time the options expire—which may or may not be good for the shareholders or the business in the long term.

Another form of phantom ownership happens in large corporations. Ownership gets too diffused to matter. This makes it hard to truly care about the company.

But in a small company where you own 30% of the company, that's your life. You're all in. Your attitude is different. You think long-term. You think about growing your wealth because it's *your* wealth—it's personal.

You may wonder, "What about a company that has less family ownership, but their name is on the corporation?"

There's an old expression called the "Idiot Son Syndrome."* The next generation doesn't always have the same business acumen as the parent or the founder, so the wealth-compounding machine grinds down.

The number of people who were on the *Forbes* list of the 400 wealthiest Americans in 1982 and are still on the list is shockingly small. So many families don't sustain whatever got them to that level of wealth.

If the family name is on it, you have to look deeper to see if the cultural values have been transmitted to the next generation. They don't have to be family members to feel that the company is their own and to run it well.

So do your homework and ask: Who owns this company?

---

* I used to joke with my dad about this.

A Case Study in Excellence: Nestlé

Nestlé is one of our current favorites. Ironically, it is too large and too dispersed to have a single owner. Yet its leadership has consistently behaved like owners. That and the following factors in our analysis have led to our enthusiasm:

Nestlé is the one of the world's largest branded food companies. The brand has built up over decades. It's not simple to start a brand and create that credibility.

Nestlé's has over 30 brands that each generates a billion dollars in sales annually.

Nestlé sells food all over the world.

People like to eat branded products because it's something they trust. They know if they liked it last time, they'll like it this time. There's a consistency of quality and safety with the products.

Nestlé has a terrific balance sheet and conservative accounting.

Nestlé is a good capital allocator and aggressively bought back stock in 2008–2009 when the stock was down. It was one of the few companies savvy enough to do that.

Then, Nestlé switched gears. When interest rates were very low, it bought companies. It bought the baby food division of Pfizer when debt was cheap. It was smart, long-range thinking: "Here's an asset that fits. Here's our chance to buy it and finance it with cheap debt. We can carry a little more debt to get this deal done. Then, we'll pay it down over time."

So in 2008–2009, when Nestlé's stock went from $60 to $40 per share, I wasn't afraid. I knew people would keep consuming Nestlé products. The question just became, "Should we be buying more?"

THE MANIC DEPRESSIVE PSYCHOLOGY OF THE MARKET

Market Volatility

John Mauldin of Millennium Wave Investment has said that, over the last century, the stock market* has been far more volatile than most investors believe.

1. From 1900 to 2002, the annual change for the Dow Jones Industrial Average reflected an average gain of 7.2% per year. As an average, this sounds mild. However, during those 103 years:

   - 63% of the years reflected positive returns. Hence, 37% were negative.

   - 1 out of 3 years was a down year.

   - The stock market either increased or decreased by more than 10% for 70% of the years.

   - The stock market index ended either up or down more than 16% for one third of those 103 years.

Given this volatility, your investment program must take into account the inevitable ups and downs of the market. Here's where the value investing approach is most valuable. In fact, the success of this approach depends on such volatility as it seeks to buy what is low and sell what is high.

---

* When I say "the market," I mean the S&P 500, but the principles here would apply to any large-scale market as well.

Mr. Market

Benjamin Graham said to imagine you have a business partner named Mr. Market, who is a reasonable guy but is subject to manic-depressive bouts.

Mr. Market is the psychology of investing.

Every day, Mr. Market prices thousands of businesses, and he's impartial. You may sell or buy as you see fit.

Most of the time, he is on the mark. He's rational enough that prices tend to reflect the underlying value.

Thankfully, there are days when he's not so sensible and is manic depressive (which he was in 2008-2009). On those days, he'll say, "Please, please, take my business from me. I'll take almost any price. Get me out of here."

When he's willing to sell at a ridiculously reduced price, you should say, "That's a good deal. I'll help you out," and buy his shares.

The key is to keep your wits about you and say, "This is a great business. Things are murky right now, but over 5 or 10 years, they'll be fine." That'll put you in the right frame of mind to be a successful investor for the long run.

There'll be times when Mr. Market is ecstatic about prospects for business. He'll plead, "Please, let me buy it from you. I will pay you the moon for your stock because I've got to have it right now." Those are moments for you to say, "He's right. Things do look good. But everybody knows that. It's reflected in a high stock price. So now is a good time to take the money."

In this way, you're using the market as your servant rather than being manipulated by it.

Every day, the stock market offers you a menu of prices on thousands of different companies. You have options:

- "That's a high price. I'll sell you mine."

- "I think that's a fair price. But I don't want to pay a fair price. I want a cheap price, so I'm not interested."

- "That's a cheap price. I'll buy some."

If you have the perspective to separate yourself from Mr. Market, you'll be a successful investor. But most people get mixed up with him and become unduly excited and scared. They are acting in concert with our manic-depressive Mr. Market. That then undermines and sabotages their investment process.

Maximum Pessimism

If everyone around me is excited, I may be skeptical at first. But after a while, I'll want to jump on the bandwagon, too. If you're not alert to some other anchoring principles to help you remain objective, though, you can get into trouble by following the crowd.

John Templeton said that the way to make money in the market is to *buy at the point of maximum pessimism*. If you think about it, when are things low? They are low when things look bad and people are scared.

I had to work on myself with this. I would get scared and become reactionary, too. That's where numeracy comes in. I have to take a deep breath and ask myself questions such as, "How cheap is it, really?" Sometimes it's not that cheap. Coming down from very high to high feels like a big drop, but it's not enough. Other times, a stock becomes an obvious bargain, it's time to get serious. It's time to step past your fear and buy.

Taking Mr. Market's Temperature

How is Mr. Market feeling? If he's riddled with fear and concern about the future, that could be a good time to go bargain hunting. If Mr. Market is feeling optimistic and excited about the future, that leads to a market that's less interesting from a value perspective. So getting a read on the psychology of Mr. Market is helpful. Howard Marks, co-founder of Oak Tree Capital Management, calls this "taking the temperature of the market."

There are numerous "thermometers" you can use to take the temperature of the market, including the media, buzzwords, the motivation of others, buybacks, mergers and acquisitions, spin-offs, fund flows, and insider trading.

The Media

The first thing I like looking at when taking the temperature of the market is the media. How is the media describing the market?

If *Time* magazine, *Fortune*, and *Barron's* say it's a great time to buy, it's too late. Most of the good opportunities have already passed.

Often the media continues to harp on about bad news—after everything that can go wrong has already gone wrong. That's a great time to be an aggressive buyer.

If a stock goes up on bad news, that's a great signal to buy. It's a sure sign that all those who were scared or angry have already sold. All that's left are people like us who say, "That's cheap, and I think all the bad news is out."

After a long period of bad news, when more bad news no longer lowers the price, that could be an opportunity.

Conversely, when the media are full of stories about how well things are going for a company, people tend to assume that it's a guaranteed success. Typically, they focus only on what could go right rather than thinking critically.

That's when I get worried and concerned.

Be wary of the sure things that magazines promote. Magazines exude confidence because it helps sell magazines to an uncertain public.

On the front cover of *Money* magazine in 2000 was an article on stocks for the next decade. It featured all the internet favorites—Cisco, Intel, and so on. Within two years, the prices of those companies' stocks were down by 80%.

Buzzwords

Keep your ears perked for buzzwords like "dot-com." It is amazing how a hot phrase gets into the public mindset. With Google, you can even track the number of times particular buzzwords are used. When buzzwords get hot and valuations get high, that's a good time to be cautious.

The Motivation of Others

There are all sorts of non-rational or non-investment motivations for selling:

- They need the cash to pay off other debts that are coming due. So they need to liquidate something.

- It's a pension fund, and it owns shares in a company that eliminates its dividend. The pension's charter does not allow owning non-dividend paying stock, so the pension fund must sell.

- It's an index fund, and the stock gets de-listed from the S&P 500 Index, so they have to sell it because it's not in the index anymore.

Being alert to the motivations of others can be helpful in explaining the market's behavior and how you should react.

Buybacks

When corporations buy back shares at an undervalued price, it increases shareholder value. However, if corporations pay a premium to buy in shares, they destroy shareholder value.

Surprisingly, buyback activity is an inverse indicator. The more companies buy back stock, the less likely it's a good time to invest.

Buybacks were huge in 2006 and 2007 during the market buildup. Then, in 2008 and 2009, the crash happened. Precisely when companies should have accelerated buybacks, they stopped! They panicked like everyone else. As a group, corporate America is not good at buybacks.

Mergers and Acquisitions

Mergers and acquisitions are when companies buy or combine with other companies.

Mergers and acquisitions ebb and flow with the temperature of the market. When markets are down, mergers and acquisitions activity slows. When markets are up, mergers and acquisitions activity picks up.

Spin-offs

Spin-offs are the inverse of acquisitions. Instead of buying something in, you're splitting something off. A corporation removes a subsidiary and sends it out into the world as a separate standalone company.

It can be a by-product of mergers and acquisitions. If the acquired company isn't working out well or is an embarrassment, a corporation spins that company off.

Sometimes you have a subsidiary that's doing well, and it's not reflected in the parent's stock market valuation. By creating a separate entity where all the focus is on that successful subsidiary, you can get a much higher price—particularly when the market is in a good mood.

So what do spin-offs say about the temperature of the market? They're done only when people are excited and feeling positive about the market. Why? When the newly independent company gets priced, it wants a good price. Spin-offs are hard to do when markets are depressed.

Fund Flows

Fund flows track where people are putting their money.*

If investors, en masse, run to invest in one specific area, it drives the market up. It may be a sign that the market is overvalued. You may want to step aside.

---

* This is well tracked in the mutual fund world by Morningstar.

If investors flee (i.e., sell) a specific investing area, the market will drop. That could be a place to do some bargain hunting.

Insider Trading

You can track insider transactions because they're reported to the Securities and Exchange Commission (SEC).

In our search to buy great companies at bargain prices, insider purchases tell a lot.

There's only one reason for insiders to buy shares. They think their stock is going up. If the whole executive team is buying, that's a strong sign.

A rush of insider buying in a long depressed industry can be a sign that the stock price is as low as it's going to go.

On the other hand, insider selling is not as clear a signal. Insiders could be selling for a lot of non-business reasons. A director could sell her shares for personal reasons (to buy a house, pay college bills, diversify her estate, and so on).

But if people in the same industry are selling en masse, that's a strong sign they believe their stock is overvalued. When executives across an entire industry are selling their shares, it's a good bet that the industry is uniformly overvalued and may be headed for a fall.

Technology insiders were selling in droves from 1999 to 2000. If insiders at Microsoft, Intel, Qualcomm, Dell, Oracle, and the like were selling, why would anyone be buying? Even more telling was that they were selling after 50% to 90% declines in their stock prices. Insiders were dumping the very same tech stocks the public was clamoring to buy. This information helped us steer our clients clear of the tech bubble.

There are two exceptions to note here.

First, it's possible for manipulative executives to purchase shares to try to influence the stock price. Dennis Kozlowski, of Tyco infamy, made a multimillion dollar purchase of Tyco shares to stem a stock free-fall. Billions of dollars of market value were destroyed by the accounting shenanigans he perpetrated.

Another exception is routine selling of shares every month by an insider. A CEO may have a planned selling program to sell equal amounts over time. This is an honorable way for a CEO to divest himself or herself, as he or she is not picking a price.

Perhaps the most noteworthy insider activity is inactivity. I have special admiration for great owner managers, such as Warren Buffett of

Berkshire Hathaway and George Joseph of Mercury General, who have never sold a share. Both men's passion is growing the intrinsic value of the enterprise—largely because it is their enterprise. More than that, it's their life's work. When you feel that way about your company, why would you sell?

Don't Lose — Part 2: What Could Go Wrong?

When looking for bargains, don't try to get a dollar of value for the price of 97 cents. Try to get a dollar for 50 cents. You want a big gap between what you're paying and what you're getting. That's called the "margin of safety."

With the ecolate filter, our corollary question was, "What could go wrong?" The answer is "Everything."

Remember, Rule #1 is "Don't lose."

You want a significant margin of safety to allow for accidents, worse-than-average luck, and miscalculation. That margin protects you just like the emergency cash fund I previously discussed.

As diligent as I've been in investing, it's amazing how many things can still fly apart. When it comes to business, you cannot make the list long enough. A large margin of safety isn't a surefire protection. It can, however, help lessen the impact of worse-than-average luck.

Warren Buffett thinks about what can go wrong better and more deeply than anyone I've ever seen. He structures his businesses to withstand great adversity and even profit under the most dire of circumstances.

For example, when Hurricane Katrina happened, the insurance industry was hit hard, but Buffett's insurance companies, as a whole, made money.

This was a stunning outcome. Buffett's companies took their lumps from that event, but because Berkshire's broad-based insurance operation earned money in other places unaffected by the hurricane, those diverse income streams offset the losses from the hurricane. Also, Berkshire is bigger than just insurance. So the utility business made money. The manufacturing companies made money. As a whole, the organization thrived in the midst of a hurricane.

Think deeply about what could go wrong and adjust your affairs so that you can weather whatever comes, and you will be well on your way to a lifelong wealth-building process.

The Danger of a Sound Premise

Benjamin Graham said, "You can get into far more trouble with a sound premise than with an unsound premise."

When I first heard this quote, it seemed nonsensical. Isn't the whole point of investing with a sound premise the avoidance of trouble? But upon further reflection, it made perfect sense. This is what happens in bubbles.

If I suggested to you that we should build a beachfront hotel in Alaska, you would dismiss the idea immediately as ridiculous (and probably dismiss me as your financial adviser). No money lost there. On the other hand, if I suggested to you that we build a beachfront hotel in Florida, you might be interested. There's sunshine year-round. It has beautiful sand beaches. The premise appears sound. Yet, millions of dollars were lost in Florida land speculation in the 1980s precisely because the premise was sound.

The sound premise was the hook that lured otherwise sensible people to choose greed over reason. They invested in unseen condos sold by seedy real estate developers. Individual building projects may have made sense individually, but taken collectively, they became an economic disaster. That's the danger of a sound premise.

One of the virtues of value investing is its focus on loss avoidance. Investments make sense only when the price paid is far below the underlying value. Thus, value investing properly applied helps to protect the investor from the excesses that can arise from a sound premise.

That concept has helped me many times.

For example, in 1998, it was sound to think "the internet will change the world" (which it has). But it is a risky leap to say, "Therefore, this stock will make me money." The truth with technology, in particular, is that often it doesn't work out for shareholders. It changes the world, but the benefits often go to the consumer, not the businesses.

A perfect example of a sound premise in recent years is 3D printing ("3D printing will change the world"). So people are investing in mom-and-pop 3D printer corporations. It's clearly a cool technology that will disrupt many businesses. And because it's so cool, it's attracting huge, well-entrenched competitors that could take over the market. But it's too early to know which companies will be successful.

Innovations Don't Always Yield Dividends

Buffett has said that there's a big difference between identifying a growth industry and making money. He has cited the airline and auto industries as examples of huge growth industries where few got rich.

Here's a personal example of where I saw this in action:

Years ago, PCA International ran photo studios in K-Mart stores. Sears had CPI. JC Penney had Landmark. All three retail chains—primary competitors—provided customers the opportunity to get their photos taken.

Then, the digital camera came along and changed the experience. With film, the customer had to wait a few weeks to get the proofs and order the photos they desired. The whole experience took a month or two. With digital cameras, the customer viewed the photos immediately after they were taken and could purchase prints on the spot.

It seemed clear that digital cameras would change the photo-buying experience. Because the cost of production was so much lower, I figured that stores would cut their prices and still widen their margins.

As it turned out, these companies figured they could cut their costs a lot and expand their market. To be competitive, they had to cut more than the competition. When the smoke cleared from the ensuing price war, they had restructured the pricing and obliterated the margin of improvement. If they had all played nice, it would have worked out well. But in the end, no one benefited.

I was disappointed, but the experience provided a great lesson. It's essential to be clear about who will benefit from the changes in technology. In this instance, it clearly accrued to the customers. They got a much better service at a much lower price. It was a win for the customers but not good for me as a shareholder. I got my money back, but it wasn't the grand success I expected.

Going Outside Your Circle of Competence

Understanding the business is primary.

In 1999, Buffett noted that there was a lot of money to be made in telecommunications by those who understood it. But he abstained because he wasn't in that group. Walter Scott, a Berkshire board member, tried to explain the industry to him, Buffett felt he had no special insight into it. Buffett had the humility and the honesty to say, "I don't understand."

We all have areas where we have a particular interest, know professionals in the business, and information and insight about how the business works. That's your circle of competence. You can say, "That's in my wheelhouse. I understand that industry and that business."

But there will be lots of companies that aren't in your circle of competence. In these cases, it would be realistic to say, "Well, I don't understand them. I think I'll pass." That's a key part of "Don't lose."

Be honest and realistic in your self-appraisal of your knowledge of the business. Is it actually within your circle of competence?

One of the big mistakes this principle helped us to avoid was Enron. Enron was one of those stocks everyone thought they had to own in the 1990s.

Corey and I looked hard at Enron because the utility industry was deregulating. If there's an ongoing fundamental shift in an industry, it can create unexpected winners. We were looking for the less-than-obvious beneficiaries of deregulation.

Enron was portraying itself as that kind of company. However, Enron's accounting was the most complex and convoluted we had ever seen. For us, that meant one of two things: either they were incredibly smart (way smarter than we are) or the accounting was fraudulent.

Corey is a sophisticated MBA/CPA from the audit department at Berkshire. So if he says, "This is totally opaque," it's totally opaque. That's why our recommendation was "Stay away. We don't know if it is good or bad. We don't trust the accounting because we don't understand it. If we can't understand it, we can't determine its value."

Here's one caveat to the idea of the circle of competence: You'll never know everything. Fortunately, with value investing, you don't need to. Practiced over time with the proper margin of safety, you produce a good return with the occasional mistake.

Being a bit of a perfectionist, I'd say with every company I've ever owned, at some level, I've felt like an impostor. I can't possibly know everything there is to know about a business, the industry it's in, and its competitive factors. I don't know it all, but I think I know enough.

That's dicey. Then something happens, and you find out you didn't know enough. "Oh crap! Now what do I do?" That's a routine experience. It's a humbling business. But that's also what makes it so exciting and satisfying when you get it right.

Moats and Obsolescence

A moat is a business advantage that makes it difficult for others to compete with you: brand, scale innovation, and so on. A moat allows you to earn higher than average returns on capital.

Buffett loves great companies with big moats. He calls great companies "first liens against the passage of time." I love that phrase. He's looking for companies that are protected from changes over time. However, the two companies he cited as examples of this in 1990 were Coca-Cola and the *Washington Post*.

Buffett noted that Coca-Cola's brand recognition worldwide was remarkable. Even its unique bottle shape was identifiable.

As things have evolved, Coca-Cola still has a great brand name and global distribution. But the idea of drinking sugar water has come into disfavor worldwide. Mexico has imposed a soda tax. People today have a different view about drinking Coca-Cola products. Although about a third of its products are non-carbonated beverages, two-thirds still are. It's a more challenged business today than it was in 1990.

With the *Washington Post*, there was almost a complete annihilation of the old business model. The traditional newspaper has been decimated by the internet. Suddenly, content was available free online. Newspapers are today's poster child for obsolescence. I was stunned at how fast those moats collapsed.

We see examples of this every day. Businesses that once looked solid can suddenly be undercut—like watches. I usually wear a watch, but my kids don't. The cell phone is their go-to device. That same cell phone also took over many other devices, such as cameras and calculators.

At the 1999 Berkshire meeting, Munger explained that it's tricky to predict what changes in technology will do. The development of the streetcar led to the rise of the department store. Since streetcar lines were immovable, it was thought that department stores had an unbeatable position because the streetcars would take people right to their doors. Offering revolving credit and a remarkable breadth of merchandise, the department store was king. Over time, the rails remained, but the streetcars disappeared. People moved to the suburbs, which led to the rise of the shopping center and ended the dominance of department stores.

Even though they're not foolproof, look for businesses with a moat. The greater the moat, the greater the certainty and the amount of future cash flows. Also, the bigger the moat, the less you need great management. As Peter Lynch said, "Find a business any idiot could run, because eventually one will."

Bubbles

Another saboteur of the compounding process is the bubble and the bust. Bubbles forming and breaking are, by far, the most important points of market history. Yet few investment programs take this into account.

A bubble is a mindset of human social crowd behavior that leads to manic behavior.

An investment bubble is when a part of the market that people invest in has been popular for a long period, and that has caused prices to go up and up and up—to the point where the pricing of the asset becomes far removed from the actual value. A manic stage has set in. People are wildly excited. But the problem is it's only valuable because of perceived value, not because it has any inherent value.

What goes up must come down. With any bubble, a bust follows. It's a cyclical process.

Everybody who was excited is already in, but everyone else doesn't care. For people to get the money back out of their investments, they have to sell. But there's no one who wants to buy.

The prices tend to drop far faster than they went up. It's shocking how fast it comes down. It comes down with the same hysteria that it went up with, if not more, because there's now panic.

There's a sudden sobering, a sudden awareness of what the actual value is, as opposed to its perceived value. It's an "emperor has no clothes" moment.

So, taking this into account for your investing program . . .

What happens to people caught up in a bubble? They don't just lose a little. It doesn't just go down 20%. They tend to lose the majority, if not all, of their investment. It's devastating.

Seeing just how devastating shows how important it is to understand bubbles and busts. Be wary of them, and make that a centerpiece of how you think about investing for the long run.

Bubbles are a common feature of the market. They will happen, and you need to be on the outside when they do. If you're in it long enough, you'll see bubbles. They're guaranteed to happen. It's just a question of when and where. The longer you're in, the probabilities become higher that you'll participate in one.

The fact that the value approach can preserve capital in a bubble–bust market has always been a key attraction for us.

We know the old maxim to "buy low, sell high." In the abstract, it's logical. In practice, much of the investment world does the opposite.

Combining a "don't lose" approach with the idea of buying low and selling high sounds great, but I found it difficult to execute in practice. Though I was dedicated to the value approach and understood it intellectually, it took 11 years to integrate the concepts with my own emotions and make the appropriate moves.

In 1994, interest rates spiked, financial stocks were clobbered, and we finally took full advantage of that bargain-hunting opportunity.

By 1999, the internet bubble was in full bloom. Most investors were taken in by the bubble. The average tenure of mutual fund managers was less than 4 years. Without adequate experience, most investors didn't have a chance.

My grandfather Russell Pecaut started in the stock business in 1925. He had a front-row seat for the 1929–1933 market crash. His sons, Richard and Jack, experienced the 1973–1974 and 1976–1982 markets.

To some extent, the dot-com bubble was a final exam for me after 20 years in the business. With the biggest bubble in history (in dollar terms), we steered our clients through reasonably well.

If you live long enough, you'll see more bubbles.

The 101st Thing

The corollary question to ask is, "What could go wrong?" Asking that question over and over again in everything you own is helpful.

What I've found is that what can go wrong is always bigger than what my brain can conceive. I can come up with 100 things, and the 101st thing is what will happen. So I add it to the list. As the list grows, I will be less surprised and make fewer errors in judgment.

Controlled Greed: Patience is the Virtue

"The trees that are slow to grow bear the best fruit."
— Moliere

As I reflect on the lessons I've learned over the past 36 years, it becomes clear that value investing maximizes the process of compounding wealth. The trick with compounding is that it takes time. It's a matter of delayed gratification. Patience is essential if you're going to be an entrepreneurial investor.

A farmer would find it ludicrous to dig up a seed every week to check its progress. As long as the inputs— such as soil, sun, and water— are adequate, he knows the process will bear fruit in good time. There's no hurrying Mother Nature.

Similarly, the world's wealthiest individuals would find it silly to check on the stock price of their businesses every hour on the hour. As long as the inputs—such as a good business model, good owner managers, and adequate capital—are in place, they know the process will bear fruit in good time.

To succeed, the investor must have a patient mindset.

Controlled Greed

The patient mindset waits for the good opportunity that's clear and cheap. If it takes time, that's okay.

As Charlie Munger says, "Successful investing is a matter of controlled greed."

As logical as the value concept may sound, I've encountered many people with whom it does not take. For them, the approach is too boring, or they seek "higher returns."

Buffett once said, "It is extraordinary to me that the idea of buying dollar bills for 40 cents takes immediately with people or doesn't take at all. It doesn't seem to be a matter of IQ or academic training. It's the recognition or nothing."

Value investing suits the temperament of the patient and repels the restless. Given that America's wealthiest individuals are patient, long-term business owners, it pays to be patient.

Value Investing—Waiting for the Second Marshmallow

In 1970, a study was conducted with 4-year-old children in which a marshmallow was placed on a table in front of each participant. Each child was instructed that he or she could eat the marshmallow. However, if the child waited to eat it until the adult monitor returned, he or she would be given a second marshmallow. What happened?

- One-third of the children immediately ate the marshmallow.

- One-third tried to wait but lost patience and ate the marshmallow.

- One-third successfully waited for the return of the adult and received two marshmallows.

The test group was examined 10 years later.

- The children in the first group (the most impatient) were doing poorly in school and were struggling with personal relationships.

- The most patient group was doing well in school and excelled in personal relationships.

The conclusion reached was that those 4-year-olds who were most able to control their impulses were most likely to be successful 14 year olds.

What's great about the marshmallow story is that it cuts out all the other variables. You could have this marshmallow now, or you could wait and have two—can you wait?

You can watch updated versions of this study on YouTube. The kids are funny. They try to wait as they wiggle around in their seats. They play with and smell the marshmallows. They torture themselves. They're smart enough to understand the payoff, but it's still incredibly difficult for them to wait.

I'd like to say that only 4-year-olds behave this way, but most people are like this. They won't wait. They want instant gratification.

Patience is a virtue in investing. Buying a dollar for 50 cents is largely a matter of waiting for the second marshmallow.

Short-Term Media

We live in a short-term oriented culture.

The media is similarly shortsighted. Unfortunately, in response, businesses have become more shortsighted as well. Businesses often focus on quarterly earnings because if they miss a quarter, the stock can drop 20% or 30% even though the underlying value of the business probably didn't change much. Think about a business having a bad quarter selling blue jeans. Did blue jeans really change that much in the last three months?

Imagine if your parents evaluated you, as a child, like those who evaluate stocks in the short-term: You're in the second grade, and you're taking a vocabulary test. Everyone expects you to score at least 90%. If you get 85% or lower, they'll be inconsolably upset. The more mature, longer view would be that, regardless of your test score, you're learning what you need to learn. When you complete this grade, you'll be promoted to third grade. After third grade, you'll move on to fourth grade. You've got a long runway to college and the rest of your life. The vocabulary test this week is such a small piece of a bigger picture, which is that you are healthy and excited about learning as well as feeling loved and supported.

But the short-term perspective of others can yield great opportunities if you have the right mindset.

For example, I wouldn't normally ever buy Apple. It's a technology company with a higher range of valuations than I'm comfortable with. Yet it went from $700 to $400 per share in 2011 when Steve Jobs passed away. People, en masse, said, "It won't be the same company anymore."

But the financials were outstanding and the stock got cheap, so it presented almost no risk of capital loss.*

Apple was one of the best brands in the world. It had an impregnable balance sheet and a great customer base. I didn't have to know what its next innovation or product would be. It clearly wasn't quitting. So my view at that moment was that Apple was unbelievably cheap. The value

---

* A simple back-of-the-envelope analysis: With $150 of cash per share, Apple had a fortress-like balance sheet. In addition, with $50 of earnings per share, Apple was trading at just 8 times earnings. Back out the cash, and you were just paying 5 times earnings.

was so compelling that even a tech idiot like me could say, "I would absolutely own that at this price."

I wouldn't have guessed that would ever happen with Apple. Other tech companies get cheap because they're dying or becoming obsolescent. Yet with Apple, the business was good. Investors were entirely focused on fears of whether Apple would stay competitive while completely ignoring the value on the balance sheet and in the current operating businesses.

Action Does Not Equal Value

America has long admired the action-oriented rugged individualist—people like Teddy Roosevelt. In many ways, it's people of action who have made America great. But with investing, acting early and often can be self-defeating. Often, the better motto is, "Don't just do something, sit there."

As professional investors, we get paid a fee by our clients (a percentage of the assets) to do what we do.

Often people equate action with value. If you turn over the whole portfolio, they think, "You obviously are doing a lot to earn your keep." However, an active trading approach creates short-term gains taxes. If you're paying short-term gains tax all the time, the after-tax returns may be substantially less than a more conservative, patient approach.

Yet, with a patient approach, our clients could think, "You've just owned this stock for 15 years. Nothing's changed. What am I paying you guys for?"

But we didn't buy Nestlé 15 years ago with the idea that "we'll own this for 15 years, cool our heels, and collect fees from our clients." No. We listen to conference calls. We read the earnings reports. In some cases, we attend the annual meeting. We're constantly updating our evaluation and understanding of the business.

At some point, our view may shift. If the stock gets too high, we'll sell. If things change and it goes outside of our circle of competence, we'll get out. If management is behaving badly or strangely, we may need to sell. There are all kinds of things that can happen.

Should we sell Nestlé tomorrow? It may have peaked yesterday. We don't know. We'll have to keep making that evaluation.

We didn't own the stock idly for 15 years. We actively made the decision over and over again that this is something we want to own. But it can appear as if we haven't done anything.

It's a psychological mistake, then, to equate activity with value.

Nestlé is a great company. When I first invested in the stock, I didn't anticipate following its rise over the next three decades. By following the company year in and year out—seeing it change and evolve, grow into emerging markets, come out with new products, buy in stock, and so on—it's clear how they've become a world-class company.

Imagine you have 10 or 12 companies you are considering for purchase. Which ones are you going to own decades from now? Who knows?

That's what makes investing so fun and fascinating. Every business is its own unfolding story. Following that story, revising your valuations, and deciding whether to own a certain stock is the ongoing challenge of the value investor.

When to Be Impatient

Patience and impatience can co-exist. A good investor needs to know when to wait 10 years and also know what cannot wait until tomorrow.

Buffett has long-term patience. But when there's blood in the water or an investment opportunity, he's impatient. When Long-Term Capital Management crashed in 1998, Buffett put in a one-hour bid—take it or leave it.

Bill Gates had a long-term vision that took patience, too. He wasn't going to accomplish it all in a day, but he had an impatience about "here's what we need to do today to make this happen."

It's a matter of understanding what requires immediate action and what could provide big benefits in the long term.

Being Too Patient

Patience comes with a caveat. Sometimes you can be too patient. That's long been a fear of mine. For me, the hardest part about patience is the doubt. It can be hard to distinguish being early from being wrong.

I'm wrong from time to time. This is not a 100% game.

At some point, you'll have to say, "That's enough. The stock is below where it was five years ago, and things didn't work out." That's where I'm slow to pull the trigger. It's my current challenge in becoming more masterful.

It's particularly tough to buy and hold with technology companies. The history of technology is dicey. With technology companies, it's nearly a 100% fail rate. Of the big technology companies in 1990, very few are still around: IBM, Microsoft, Hewlett-Packard, and a few more. It's a short list. Thousands of companies have come and gone since then.

Strategies to Remain Patient

You may wonder, "What does it take to remain patient? How do I make myself less likely to second-guess my choices?"

In moments of doubt, it helps to have trusted allies who you can ask, "Hey, what's your take on this? What do you think about my assumptions?" Bounce ideas off them so you can hear what they think. This helps give you a more objective perspective in your more subjective moments.

My partner and I review our investments on a schedule. We have a three- to five-year map. We check it quarterly to see whether the investments are on track. We're not tied to the quarterly earnings, per se. In a general way, we ask questions such as: "Are the fundamentals of the business improving? Is the moat around the castle growing?" We keep an eye on the key variables.

You can structure your life for maximum patience, too.

If you have debt (a mortgage, a car loan, or a student loan) and you own stocks, you have, in effect, borrowed to be in the stock market. It's important to be debt free when the market fluctuates (especially in periods of extreme volatility). When the market goes down, if you own everything you own, it can't be taken from you. You won't have to sell. You're in a strong position to say, "I believe in this company, and I'll stay the course." If you have any debt, it amplifies your fear and short-term thinking. For too many people, when things go south, they get scared and liquidate their stocks at low prices. That blows up their long-term game plan.

Lastly, focus on the big picture. If you stay at this long enough, you will have a few big winners and some disastrous failures. At those times, your ego may soar or be crushed. However, the real key is to keep an even keel and maintain the focus of your overall portfolio.

BARGAIN HUNTING: SEARCHING FOR TREASURE

Now that I've covered all these topics separately, it's time to show how they combine into one approach: bargain hunting. Bargain hunting requires business analysis skills, an understanding of the market, and most of all, patience.

I spoke about having a margin of safety as a way to avoid losing. Another key piece of the margin of safety is bargain hunting. Remember, you're not looking to buy a dollar for 90 cents. You want a dollar for 50 cents. So how do you find bargains?

When the market is going down and people get scared, that's when you can buy a dollar of value for 50 cents. That's where the great bargains are. Remember Templeton: You want to buy at the point of maximum pessimism.

It's a simple idea, but it takes rigor to implement. In a world where we're taught to follow trends and do what's working for others, it's difficult to cut your own path as a value investor—but it's worth it.

First, you have to be able to analyze a business and figure out what it's worth. Then, you can look at the price and say, "Well, that's a discount," or "That's a premium." That gives you a range of where you may want to buy or sell. It helps emotionally to already know what a cheap price and a high price would be. That way you're not hostage to Mr. Market.

It doesn't have to be complicated. You just need to do some homework, develop a circle of competence, and understand the accounting so that you know what the numbers mean. Then do a valuation to know if the price is cheap.

If you have a clear understanding of what businesses are worth in a particular industry, you can create a range of value through history:

- Here's how those stocks are valued when everyone's happy.

- Here's what buyouts are going for (and, thus, what knowledgeable insiders are willing to pay).

- Here's where the group sells when people are scared and the clouds are dark.

Buffett said, "It's easier to think about what will happen rather than when." That's a valuable insight. When things are bad and are going down, the question to ask is always, "How bad is it?" You have to make your own assessment and determine whether it's a permanent diminution of value or a temporary drop that will recover.

We've had a number of situations where we agree on the facts with the people who are selling the stock. Yet, we're buying. The reason is our timeframes are longer term.

The ability to be patient and take a long view puts you at a huge advantage over the rest of the market. Your attitude about the future can create an opportunity. You don't have to know anything that other people don't. You simply take a different view: "It looks bad now, but this is a dollar selling for 50 cents. In 3 to 5 years, the clouds will pass. It'll return to its average valuation. At that price, I double my money."

You can't know everything, but you can know a few things well. Establish your circles of competence and establish your valuation: "Here's where this company's cheap. Here's where it's expensive. Here's the middle range where it'll be priced most of the time." Sometime in a three-year period, it'll hit a high or a low. That's when you want to be ready. If the stock is verifiably cheap, then you have to act.

For example, in 1990, Disney's stock went from $24 to $17. Disney was clearly one of the great franchises in the world. The Disney board was smart. They did a huge buyback at $17 a share (the stock had previously been as high as $30 a share). It was an amazingly timed bargain. For such a high-quality company to buy that much stock at such a cheap price was an unusual and hugely value-creating event. It was only created because some major stockholders' stock ownership had gotten too leveraged, and they were forced to sell at an inopportune time.

During lawsuits, companies can become overly discounted (and therefore a bargain). I remember Buffett bought Texaco bonds when Texaco declared Chapter 11 bankruptcy. Texaco wasn't really in as bad a shape as the bankruptcy made it appear. It was just in a cash flow squeeze. But that declaration of bankruptcy scared conventional bondholders, who sold bonds down to 50 cents on the dollar. Texaco wasn't out for good. It had the ability to pay eventually. When it did, Buffett made a huge profit.

It's the companies that aren't doing well that may be the more interesting ones to double down on. In those situations, ask yourself, "Is their business model still intact? Is the management still building value? Is the moat widening or shrinking?" If the answers are yes (i.e., the value is up and the stocks are down), then the potential return has increased, not decreased. It's counterintuitive, but that's how you can gain disproportionate value in the long run.

ACTION STEPS: PART TWO

Here is a distilled down summary of all the actions you can take now that you've read and understood what came before:

Clear, logical, and unemotional thinking are at the heart of any great entrepreneurial investor. Develop a solid thinking framework to stay on track. Apply Garrett Hardin's three filters to refine and improve your thinking: the literate filter ("What are the words being used?"), the numerate filter ("What are the numbers?"), and the ecolate filter ("And then what?"). Consistently apply these filters until they become integrated in your thinking and you do them naturally.

To increase your rate of wealth building, you need to own businesses. To determine which businesses you want to own, you must analyze the following aspects:

- What makes a good company?

- Which variables are most important?

- What is it worth (value)?

- What is the cost (price)?

- Is this something worth buying after you compare the price and the value?

Do the math. Forget the market while you do your analysis. Make your own judgments. Your assessment will tell you whether to buy, sell, hold, or pass. If the price is reasonable, hold it. If the price is significantly higher than what you came up with, sell it or pass. If the price is significantly lower, hold it or buy it.

Take the time to become fluent in accounting. Learn how to read a balance sheet and income statement. I recommend reading *The Interpretation of Financial Statements* by Benjamin Graham and Charles McGoldrick.

Consider how much capital the business requires to grow. Being able to grow without much capital means there'll be much more profit for you to pocket.

Also, determine whether the leaders are good capital allocators. At some point in every successful business, capital allocation becomes as important as—or more important than—the business operation. What the business does with its cash will highly impact the long-term value of the business.

When looking at companies, always ask who owns it. If their managers don't own it, you probably shouldn't own it, either. Invest in businesses where the people running it are up to their eyeballs in that business and their family's net worth is on the line.

Your investment program must take into account the inevitable ups and downs of the market. The stock market is, after all, far more volatile than most investors believe.

When Mr. Market is willing to sell at a ridiculously reduced price, you should buy his shares. Use the market as your servant rather than being manipulated by it.

As John Templeton said, *buy at the point of maximum pessimism.* Buy when are things are low, when things look bad, and when people are scared. When a stock becomes an obvious bargain, step past your fear and buy.

Take the temperature of the market. Ask how Mr. Market is feeling. Use the numerous "thermometers" available to you: the media, buzzwords, the motivation of others, buybacks, mergers and acquisitions, spin-offs, fund flows, and insider trading. If Mr. Market is riddled with fear and concern about the future, it could be a good time to go bargain hunting. If Mr. Market is feeling optimistic and excited about the future, it's a less interesting market.

Get a large margin of safety between what you're paying and what you're getting. Don't try to get a dollar of value for 97 cents. Try to get a dollar for 50 cents.

Beware of the sound premise, the hook that lures otherwise sensible people to choose greed over reason.

Innovations don't always yield dividends. It's essential to be clear about who will benefit from the changes in technology. It's often the customers and not the shareholders.

Don't go outside of your circle of competence. Invest only in those businesses you understand. There will be lots of companies that aren't in your circle of competence. Be honest and realistic in your self-appraisal of your knowledge of the business. Have the humility and honesty to say, "I don't understand."

Look for moats when choosing what businesses to own. The greater the moat, the greater the certainty and the amount of future cash flows. Also, the bigger the moat, the less great management is needed.

A major saboteur of the compounding process is the bubble and the bust. Your investment program must take bubbles into account and protect against them. Be wary of them, and make that a centerpiece of how you think about investing for the long run.

To succeed, the investor must be patient. As long as the inputs—such as a good business model, good owner–managers, and adequate capital—are in place, rest assured that the process will bear fruit in good time.

With investing, acting early and often can be self-defeating. It's a mistake to equate activity with value.

Don't idly own a stock. Actively make the decision over and over again that this is something you want to own. At some point, your view may shift. If the stock gets too high, sell. If things change and it goes outside of your circle of competence, get out. If management starts behaving badly or strangely, sell.

Patience and impatience should co-exist. Understand what requires immediate action and what could provide big benefits in the long term.

Sometimes, you can be too patient. It can be hard to distinguish being early from being wrong. You'll be wrong from time to time. At some point, you'll have to say, "That's enough. Things didn't work out."

In moments of doubt, it helps to have trusted allies who can help you test assumptions and bounce ideas off.

Review investments on a schedule to see if they are on track or not.

Structure your life for maximum patience. If you have any debt, it amplifies your fear and short-term thinking. Be debt free so you're in a strong position to stay the course with your long-term game plan.

All the topics we've discussed combine into one approach: bargain hunting. When the market is going down and people get scared, you can buy a dollar of value for 50 cents. That's where the great bargains are: at the point of maximum pessimism.

Companies can become overly discounted during a crisis. In those situations, ask yourself: Is their business model still intact? Is the management still building value? Is the moat widening? If the answer is yes (i.e. the value is up, and the stocks are down), then the potential return has increased, not decreased. It's an opportunity to gain disproportionate value in the long run.

Cut your own path as an investor. It's difficult, but it's worth it.

First, analyze a business and figure out what it's worth. Then, look at the price and decide whether it's a discount or a premium. That gives you a range of where you may want to buy or sell. It helps emotionally to already know what a cheap price and a high price would be. Then, you're not hostage to Mr. Market.

Take a long view. Make your own assessment to determine whether it's a permanent diminution of value or a temporary drop that will recover. If you have the patience to wait for it to recover, that will be a huge advantage.

You are capable of learning this process yourself, but you may want to delegate your investing to a professional. It can be valuable to have a registered investment advisor as an ally who can do those things for you.

HEAD AND HEART: GIVING WITH A BUSINESS MINDSET

Thinking back, one failing I've had was not talking to clients more about giving. I was never comfortable getting into deeper conversation or telling someone what they should do. Giving is a deeply personal act. It should be internally driven. The best I can do is show what I have done.

In the past, the most I've discussed with my clients is the idea of giving appreciated stock to a charity. When you give appreciated stock, you don't have to pay capital gains tax. When the charity receives the gift and sells the stock, it doesn't have to pay any capital gains, either. The charity gets the full value of the gift. In the end, it's a win-win. You get a tax deduction, and the charity gets the gift. That was the most I've shared with my clients before this.

I've been private about my own giving. This book is the first time I've put it all out there. I don't want it to come off as bragging in any way, but rather as an encouragement for others. The impact we can make with our giving is 10 times what we think we can make. There's a step change available if you grow your own capacities and awareness around giving and money.

This adult phase of my giving life, long after the dime in the church's collection plate, started in 1987. It happened when I traveled to the Bahamas to meet with one of my investing heroes, John Templeton.

Everything unfolded naturally from there.

JOHN TEMPLETON TOLD ME TO TITHE

1987 marked a big shift in my understanding about giving. My wife, Kay, and I traveled to the Bahamas with a group of professional investors to meet with one of my investing heroes, John Templeton.

We met with him in his mahogany-paneled office in Lyford Cay. He was as gracious and dignified as I had hoped. But he surprised me by showing genuine curiosity about where we came from and what we were doing. He had low ego. It wasn't all about him.

When it came time for him to discuss investing, he, in essence, said, "I want to share an investment with you that guarantees a dramatic return. Everyone I've seen do this has done well. Not just well, but phenomenally well." My mouth was watering. My pen was ready. He had me hooked. He said, "That investment is tithing."*

I recall thinking, "Huh?" I knew he was religious, but it still surprised me. I was looking for investment advice in a monetary sense.

According to Templeton, tithing is like magic. Good fortune entered his life in unexpected ways when he chose to tithe. His life improved when he started tithing. He said he has never met anyone who had tithed and regretted it. That sold me: It was never a negative for anyone to tithe.

It was miraculous that Kay was in the room. She has never accompanied me to a business meeting before or since. But she was there in the room that day. It felt like she was meant to hear it with me.

We discussed it and decided, "Well, let's go for it."

First, I measured what we were already giving. Remember, what gets measured gets done. I wasn't measuring just my giving. I was measuring many things: my income, my progress at work, our revenues at work, our expenses at work, and so on. But I was conveniently not measuring

_____

* Tithing means giving away one-tenth of your income for the good of others.

my giving. I considered myself a generous guy, but when I looked, we were giving only 2% of our income. Tithing is 10%. Yikes. It was going to be a bigger leap than I expected.

We jumped from 2% to 10% overnight. We didn't do it incrementally. We jumped off the cliff.

We had three kids. Kay had quit her job at the post office to be a full-time mom. I was buying ownership in Pecaut & Company to become a partner. It made no economic sense whatsoever to increase our giving.

Soon, we got to a place where we wouldn't have enough money to make it through the month. We'd run out. We had increased our giving five-fold, but nothing else changed. Obviously, the budget would run off track.

Magically, our tax refund came the next week. We'd sent the tax return in, it was processed, and the check was mailed back to us far quicker than could be expected. It didn't seem possible. But it happened, and we got through the month. We both took it as a sign to keep going.

Tithing seemed insurmountable at first. But after passing that trial, it quickly became integrated into our lives.

BECOMING LESS ATTACHED TO MY GROWING WEALTH

My sister was in the Peace Corps in Mauritania 20 years ago. When we visited her, she coached us that the locals would offer us gifts even though they lived in abject poverty and had few worldly possessions. She said, "The gracious thing to do is to receive it and say 'Thank you.' Do not give it back. That would be an embarrassment."

It was humbling to have people invite us into their homes to sit on a dirt floor and share a meal. The standard meal was a bowl of couscous and goat meat. They would also throw a vegetable or two in there (which was a big deal because those were hard to come by). They gave us beautifully dyed, ornate, handcrafted pillows to sit on and served tea in a silver tea set. They always gave the nicest things they owned to their guests.

Although my sister had prepared us, the experience stunned me. I realized, "Wow! I'm not a sharer. I am way more attached to my stuff. How much more freedom would there be if I were a little less attached?"

Studies show that as people get wealthier, they tend to become more attached to their wealth. The more income a person makes, the lower percentage of that income, on average, he or she gives. The wealthier we become, the more attached we become to what we think we have.

The magic of tithing is that it puts a little crowbar in that attachment and loosens it up a bit. It helped me realize, "This isn't all about me. This money isn't even mine. When I die, it goes back into the world. Who am I kidding?"

Giving expanded my awareness of others and the needs of the world.

Small Gifts, Large Impact

Microlending is a significant way to give at a smaller level. Microlending is a small loan to a small business in a developing country. Donating $25 or $50 helps a person who cannot otherwise get financing to start or grow their businesses. It may not seem like much to you, but it can be a step change for that person's life or community.

It's become an increasingly popular idea with the internet and services like Kiva.com.

I anticipated the current microlending trend on that trip to Mauritania 20 years ago. I thought, "There are no banks here. So when people need capital, what can they do? There's nothing there. There's no infrastructure. Unless you have an uncle with some money, what do you do?" My sister agreed to be the loan officer, and I gave her a few thousand dollars. I told her to find people of quality who have a good idea or plan, and to go for it.

She found Mohammed, a young go-getter with a cab. That worked well until the cab broke down. One guy had a kiln to make pots. I liked that one. It seemed self-sustaining. My favorite entrepreneur was a man who bought a donkey and a cart to haul water from the well to the village. It was a much-needed service. Money came in from him every month. He was paying his loan back. Then, one day, the payments stopped. Eventually, the man mailed my sister a letter saying that the donkey had died. So that was that. That was as far we went with microlending in Mauritania.

Even though it lasted only a short time, the experience made me aware of how we take infrastructure for granted. Getting something done without a supportive infrastructure is exceedingly difficult. We take it for granted in America. That doesn't exist for much of the world.

I became aware of how big an impact a small amount of capital can make.

My First Large Gift: The Dorothy Pecaut Nature Center

Kay and I made our first large gift in 1997. This was 10 years into my tithing. The gift was my dad's idea. My mom had just passed away, and he wanted us, as a family, to make a naming gift for a new local nature center. My household's contribution would be $50,000.

I was in mourning and was uncomfortable with the idea. I was resistant. My resistance wasn't just about the money. It was that my mom was low key. I thought she wouldn't want her name on something. But my dad was clear and showed a lot of leadership.

Kay and I agreed to go in for our share. So, as a family, we made a large naming gift for what became the Dorothy Pecaut Nature Center.

It's been such a beautiful thing. My mom loved kids and nature. Now, tens of thousands of kids have gone through the center and learned all kinds of things about nature, camping, and hiking. It's what she loved. It's a perfect way for her to be remembered.

I appreciate my dad's wisdom. I would never have thought of something like that. It opened my eyes to the fact that well-made large gifts can make a big difference and bring value to the community.

Measuring for Maximum Impact

Whether large or small, I want to make a difference and have an impact with what I do.

I pay attention to the impact of my giving and whether it is effective.

I've served on quite a few non-profit boards over the years. I've seen so much dysfunction (organizations that did not have budgets or apply a numerate world view). There were also a lot of politics, regulation, and relational issues.

I want my money, time, and effort to make a difference. I want an operation that works. That's hard to find.

Once again, what gets measured gets done. I measure the impact:

- How effectively and efficiently is it in delivering an impact?

- Is the entity focused on the mission and the steps needed to complete its goal?

- Is the management being evaluated regularly?

Essentially, I take the investment mindset and apply it to giving. I search for good organizations just as I would search for good businesses. Then I hold them to delivering results.

GOODWILL: AN ENTREPRENEURIAL NON-PROFIT

A major lesson on social entrepreneurship came to me through Goodwill Industries, an organization dedicated to helping people find dignity through work. More specifically, it came to me through our local branch, Goodwill of the Great Plains.

Each region of Goodwill has a certain amount of autonomy to run its programs in its own way and to choose which additional services to offer.

Thirteen years ago, I joined the board of Goodwill of the Great Plains. I found John Hantla, the CEO, to be a good, honest, and transparent person. But Goodwill lacked modern management systems. It lacked a vision for growth beyond what it was already doing.

At the time, our local branch had $11 million in revenues with 13 stores. There was room for a lot more stores in the region, but we would need deeper leadership if it was going to grow to its full potential. Hantla was smart enough to realize this.

Hantla encouraged the board to set several initiatives:

- Double the size of our business. We could easily have 20 or more stores in the service area.

- Develop leadership, particularly younger leadership (I didn't understand just how important this would be).

- Become self-funding. This was essential as it was clear that state and federal government budgets would become increasingly stretched.

It's amazing how that organization has transformed over the last 13 years. Revenue went from $10 million to over $20 million. The store count went from 13 to 22. The stores are better and more efficient. Store managers were measured on what they did and got bonuses when they hit their marks.

Our team developed leadership programs that are moving throughout the organization. At one point, Goodwill of the Great Plains had five young people in leadership programs. Today, it has 40. Both the head of operations and the head of leadership development are in their 30s. The organization has talented people advancing throughout. Goodwill has evolved into a leadership development organization.

The beauty of it is our Goodwill's fundamental model hasn't changed. It is a great business model: The cost of selling donated goods is low. Its main cost stems mostly from sorting and cleaning donated goods. The net profit from the items sold in the stores is the primary funding for the organization and its services.

To augment cash flows, our Goodwill also expanded its grant writing and charitable giving programs.

With these cash flows, Hantla's team acts as social entrepreneurs. Programs are reviewed for impact, efficiency, and relevance to the mission. With limited resources, time, and talent, it's important to focus. We say no to programs that no longer work, have unreliable funding, or duplicate existing efforts. We let those things go. Then that creates space to try something new. Some initiatives have failed, but we always learned from our mistakes. We became proactive in making each dollar work harder.

Three new programs have especially been home runs: YouthBuild, the Connection Center, and the Achievement Center.

#1—YouthBuild

There is data that shows if people don't find gainful employment between the ages of 18 and 26, it'll be difficult for them to get their lives turned around. YouthBuild gives those at-risk youth a real chance at success.

YouthBuild is a federal government program that helps at-risk high school students complete their high school equivalencies, get diplomas, and learn job skills (typically in the building trade). They gain the satisfaction, dignity, and self-confidence of work.

YouthBuild is so popular now that Goodwill has a waiting list. The word has gotten out that this is a program that can help kids get their lives on track.

Habitat for Humanity partners with YouthBuild, so it's also helping people in need of housing in the process. It dovetails well with other services in this area.

YouthBuild is clearly a winner. Unfortunately, in some places, Youth-Build is no longer offered because government funding has run out. However, our Goodwill has the ability to fund that program because of its cash-generating capabilities. And so it has. This is the social entrepreneurial approach that the organization can now take.

#2—Connection Center

The primary mission of Goodwill is putting people to work. The slogan is "Donate stuff, create jobs."

Our Goodwill region now has nine stores with Connection Centers. These centers help people looking for work find a job. The Connection Center team helps them create resumes, do skills assessments, participate in job fairs, and apply for jobs online. The Connection Center can help bring employers and potential employees together.

There is joy and satisfaction that comes out of doing work. There's dignity. There's a sense of connection with the people you work with. Empowerment and well-being come with a well-earned paycheck.

However, there are significant portions of the population that find it difficult to get into the workplace. Veterans and immigrants are two growing groups in need of assistance. That's been a big shift over the last decade.

A lot of people are willing to work and have skills, but they don't know how to get into the system. That's where the Connection Center comes in.

We have the ability to do skills assessment and training. We set up an environment where the job meets the person where they are. Helping those with mental and physical disabilities is one of our strong suits.

The growth has been amazing. Thirteen years ago, Goodwill of the Great Plains was placing 50 to 75 people to work a year. In 2014, 1,500 people were put to work. In 2015, we expect over 1,800 will be put to work through our Connection Centers. The numbers are hard to be firm on, but it looks like 1 out of 4 job hirings in our city last year were facilitated by the Goodwill system.

There's no question that this is the most effective innovation in Goodwill I've ever seen. It's a game changer. I am amazed at the level of efficiency and effectiveness at which our Goodwill is operating.

#3—Achievement Center

Building the Achievement Center at our Goodwill camp was another project that showed how much more dynamic our Goodwill was becoming.

We have the only Goodwill camp in the country. For over 80 years, kids below the poverty line and kids with disabilities have been able to go to camp through this program. But, over the years, the camp had become run down.

Over the last 15 years, the organization has been rebuilding the camp and updating its facilities. One big update was a new swimming pool facility that has a ramp so kids in wheelchairs can experience the water, which can be quite a powerful experience.

The crowning jewel in this refurbishment process was the vision to have an Achievement Center. It would be a large building with its own kitchen and meeting rooms where people could gather. It was called the Achievement Center because it could host award ceremonies and banquets.

John Hantla had envisioned building this achievement center for some time. Jan Paulson, the Board Chair, had approved it. However, with the sub-prime crash in 2009, I was dubious about the timing. I loved the idea, but questioned whether it was the best time to raise funds for a $2.5 million project. Thankfully, Paulson and Hantla presented the idea to the board, which eventually, after much deliberation, said yes.

I'm proud of how it all came out. It illustrates the proactive behavior of the whole organization. Even though the general economy and the markets were down, we went ahead with a game-changing project.

The camp is now in demand by outside groups. It has becoming a year-round facility rather than just a summer facility. The state-of-the-art kitchen was used by a local community college to give culinary classes. It shifted the camp from being a private property for Goodwill programs to something the whole community can see as a resource.

The Big Picture

None of these three programs existed at Goodwill five years ago. This is the power and potential impact of having a social entrepreneurial organization that's extremely well run on the business side.

The thrift store operation diverts 17 million pounds of waste from landfills every year. When I got involved, 15% to 20% of all the goods received went to the landfill. Today, it's down to 7%. What's not sold through the stores is sold for salvage.

We've created this dynamic organization with the capacity to innovate. What I'm excited about is that the best innovations are yet to come. Goodwill of the Great Plains is now aiming to be a $30 million organization. Even though it would be more comfortable to do what we've done before, pushing beyond our current boundaries is exciting. This experience has changed my view of how powerful it can be to carry the principles of impact, innovation, and leadership development into the realm of social enterprise.

THE MANKIND PROJECT: AN ORGANIZATION ON THE ROPES

The ManKind Project (MKP), an international personal development organization, now in its 30th year, was started by Rich Tosi, Bill Kauth, and Ron Herring. They saw women getting involved with the feminist movement and wondered why men weren't redefining their roles in society as well.

Men in our culture are trained to be emotionally repressed or in denial, which creates a lot of confusion and problems. Getting in touch with emotions and getting *the information in the feelings* can bring great insight, healing, and clarity for men.

So they developed this crazy initiation weekend for men called the New Warrior Training Adventure. It knocked people's socks off. It's been tuned up over the years, but the fundamentals remain the same. About 40,000 men have attended these weekend trainings.

In addition to the weekends, thousands of men sit in MKP circles every week to integrate the changes and insights from the weekend. My friend David Bauerly once said, "Continuous positive change requires continuous positive support." MKP's circles and community provide that support.

Joining MKP

My friend Mark Avery mentioned the group to me 13 years ago. It was at a period in my life when I felt dead inside. I was able to function, but I wasn't able to feel joy. I felt like the system had tricked me. I had done the things I was taught to do: be a good father, a good husband, an honest business owner, and give back to the community. My life should have been thriving, but it wasn't. I felt flat and empty.

So when he recommended MKP to me, I jumped at the opportunity. I liked that I'd never heard of it. I needed something completely different. Whatever I needed, I wasn't getting. I didn't ask any questions about it. I just signed up and went on the next weekend retreat.

It was fantastic. It took my life from black and white to Technicolor like in *The Wizard of Oz*. It gave me emotional awareness. What I learned was that, if I want to feel joy deeply, then I need to feel my pain deeply. Joy, anger, sadness, and fear are a package deal. I couldn't cut off one emotion and expect to feel another. I also realized that I never knew how to grieve my mother's death. That's where things were stuck for the next five years. I don't think I would have ever found out those things without that weekend, but it was what I needed to break through.

The initial weekend opened up the door: here's Technicolor. But it could have slammed shut again if I didn't continue to integrate the changes. The weekly groups gave me a chance to go over the patterns that didn't serve me and consciously change them into patterns that would.

The Analysis

About five years ago, it became clear that the organization had outgrown its grassroots beginnings. It had gone about as far as it could as a volunteer organization, and it was failing. MKP was trying to operate on fees from trainings with men working their tails off, getting paid a fraction of what they should to do things they weren't trained for. Basic operational functions were not being handled properly. It wasn't anyone's fault. It was that the proper structure wasn't in place.

In the midst of this failing, Bruce Maxwell, a Stanford MBA and graduate of the weekend, saw the value of MKP and knew it needed a lifeline. He went to the MKP leadership and said that Stanford had a special program through which its alumni did pro bono work. He suggested that MKP apply to the program. If accepted, he and his team would prepare an in-depth business plan for MKP. The MKP leadership was delighted and filled out the application. Happily, MKP was accepted.

Maxwell, along with four other Stanford MBA graduates, did beautiful work. If MKP had paid for an equivalent analysis, it would have cost hundreds of thousands of dollars.

MKP and the Stanford team researched and found about 30 organizations that were similar, in some way, to MKP. They determined what worked and what didn't work in those organizations. What didn't work was funding an organization with fees from trainings. The fail rate for that approach was 100%. So MKP had lasted as long as it did because of the passion of its volunteers—not because of the structure.

MKP was failing. Enrollments had peaked in 2005. That was good because it gave us clarity and urgency that we had to do something. The house was on fire, and they had to get moving.

Here's what Maxwell and his team suggested should happen. First, MKP needed a professional headquarters, including a professional executive director, treasurer, and IT and marketing directors. In addition, MKP needed professional systems to track and evaluate what it was doing.

Secondly, MKP needed more funding sources. Maxwell and his team recognized that MKP had 32 centers across the country—each an independent corporation. If MKP could consolidate those centers all under one corporation and file one tax return, it would be more efficient.

In addition, many of the 32 centers had a little slush fund for unexpected expenses. In our local center, for example, we had $15,000 in reserve just in case. We never actually tapped into it while I was involved. For MKP nationally, this represented an important yet untapped resource—about $500,000 of mostly idle funds across all those centers. Consolidating these funds would create capital that could be invested in building MKP.

In addition, Maxwell and his team suggested that MKP develop a membership-funding program. Today, MKP has a membership program with 3,000 members. If membership gets to be over 6,000 members, the membership program alone would largely fund the operation.

Third, Maxwell and his team saw that MKP could roll out new and innovative trainings to the whole world. This would extend our mission and create new revenue streams.

If implemented, this whole transition would transform MKP from an inward-looking, grassroots volunteer organization to an outward-looking, mission-based organization with technology, accountability, well-run finances, and high-quality professional talent at all levels.

My Part in This Transformation

When Maxwell and the Stanford team presented this plan, it initially caused fear and angst in the organization. MKP had a bias against anything corporate or bureaucratic.

Maxwell built consensus among regional centers by traveling all over the country on his own dime to present the plan and get feedback.

He got lots of heat from men who were worried about this new direction. But by being heard, they were able to accept the new game plan, albeit sometimes begrudgingly, in order to survive. Maxwell's consensus building was a huge gift to the whole organization.

Even with consensus, it wasn't going to be easy. The plan called for raising a $400,000 to $1 million investment fund to build the new organization. These funds would be separate from funds in the operating budget.

Eventually Jon Levitt, from Philadelphia, and I became the development committee to raise this investment fund to change the course of MKP.

We soon discovered that MKP had very weak accounting. The organization just didn't have the systems, equipment, or support to do it right. It could not even say whether it was making or losing money. Levitt moved mountains to put together proper financial statements and reporting systems.

I was naïve about the fundraising activity. I didn't think it would be that hard. I assumed that with a list of 50 successful businessmen in MKP, I could easily raise $500,000 by getting $10,000 from each of them.

As I called my list, I heard the same story almost every time. "I loved the weekend. It totally changed my life. I use the skills I learned every day. But I won't give one thin dime." This taught me two things: 1) There was universal acclaim for the quality of the weekend and the weekly groups, and 2) there was universal disdain for how the organization had handled its finances. That perspective made sense to me, so I would always say, "I agree, but this is our chance to change it. The window will close soon. Won't you jump through it with me?"

The answer was a resounding "No." Everyone was in a "show me" mode. This was good for the long term (there were a lot of potential donors), but there was so much baggage and negativity that it wasn't going to happen any time soon.

In early 2011, Levitt and I were joined by Mike Elser and Russell Kramp. Our goal was to raise at least $400,000 by June 30, 2011. If we didn't raise the full amount, we would return everything we'd raised. To answer concerns about financial integrity, we established a trust account. Kramp agreed to be the trustee so we could assure that all funds raised would go to the plan and nothing would go to the budget (which is what many men feared would happen).

By the end of February, we had raised $200,000. We were halfway there, but we were tired—$400,000 seemed like a long way away. But

Elser was brilliant. He said, "Let's move the deadline up to March 31, 2011." We were dragging, so moving the deadline up created energy.

I was stunned. I thought, "That's impossible. How the heck are we going to do that?"

Something shifted for me that night, and in the morning, the question became a personal challenge.

As I mulled the situation over, a memory from my early days at Pecaut & Company came to me. Though retired, my grandfather, Russell Pecaut, would come back in the summers and would take me to Bishop's Cafeteria for lunch. I was so excited to get my grandpa all to myself. I liked going to lunch with the founder of the firm. I felt like a big shot in my goofy little suit as I ate chocolate ambrosia pie with white meringue on top.

On one such day after we had eaten our lunch, he looked at me and said, "You know, Dan . . ." His voice changed, and the hair on the back of my neck went up. He had me on the edge of my seat.

He said, "There'll be a couple times in your life where you'll have a big decision to make, and what you do with that will change everything."

He went on and talked about how a local building, the Badgerow building, had come up for sale during the Great Depression. At the time, it was the best class A art deco building around. It was the best office space in the city, no question. He was invited to be part of a partnership that would buy it. He knew it would be a great deal. But he had a wife and young children, and it would stretch him financially. So he passed. He said a day did not go by when he saw that building and didn't regret not making that investment. As the country came out of the Depression, buying the building would indeed have been a fabulous investment.

He went on to relate that when his sons Dick (my father) and Jack graduated from college in the mid-1950s, they went into the securities business with him at C. W. Britton. In 1960, they had an opportunity to go out and start their own business, Pecaut & Company. This time he said "Yes." Because his sons were young and didn't have any capital, he took all the financial risk. Since he was in his 50s, if it didn't work, it would be tough to recover. It put him in a pickle. It was a risk, but he took it anyway since he knew it was the right thing to do. It worked out so much better than he had even hoped. They made money from day one. So that was the lesson: Be aware that there will be some big moments where your choice can make all the difference.

This was the moment that he was talking about.

"This is it. I could be the one to step up and forever change the course of this organization and take it from a grassroots organization to a world-changing one." I knew it could happen.

Then, an idea I learned from my business experience popped into my head: incentivizing. I could offer a $50,000 gift that would match up to $100,000 (50 cents on every dollar) of donations.

If we raised $100,000 that way and matched it with the $50,000, we'd be shy of $400,000, but the momentum would carry us over. It was immediately clear to me without any more analysis that this was the right way to go.

I eagerly shared the idea with the team. I wanted "the donor" to be anonymous. I didn't want it to be about me in any way.

Elser knew a guy who could create a webpage with a big red button that said "I'm in." Donors would click on it and enter their credit card information to make their gift. Then, the darnedest thing happened. It went viral. We went from a grinding four- or five-month process to suddenly having this parabolic lift. Dozens of donations came in every day.

I realized it was a referendum: "Do enough men believe in this and want it? If we don't raise the money, it's okay. It needs to die, and we'll all move on to other things. If enough men care, we'll do it all the way."

Day by day, word kept spreading through the internet, and more men were giving. We had 700 donors that last month. At midnight on March 31, 2011, the day of the deadline, we crossed $400,000.

It was dramatic. It could not have been more like a Hollywood script. If we hadn't raised at least $400,000, we would have had to give it all back. It was all-or-nothing, and we got it all.

We did something dozens of intelligent business people thought was impossible. Maxwell put together the plan with his team. Everyone followed it. Men stepped up in different ways. There's now so much excitement and passion. MKP has the direction, focus, and structure necessary to expand its impact.

Today, MKP has an excellent executive team, sound organizational structure, and thousands of members across the country. It's miles away from where we started, and the future is bright. Innovation is accelerating. We've even run online classes with students from 55 different countries.

It was such a powerful experience for me—it took me to another level. So, what else is possible?

PINE RIDGE: MAKING OF ALLIES

The Pine Ridge Reservation is where so many of these threads come together. It's also why I've decided to give the profits from this book to healing genocide (which I'll explain why).

Gustav Pecaut, my great-great-grandfather, settled in Nebraska in 1852 after emigrating from Switzerland. He was the third Caucasian settler in this area. He learned to speak some Lakota. He traded furs and led trading parties into South Dakota. He was a pioneer and a wild man. He was shot in the back with arrows over a trade disagreement. Gustav was part of the European migration that, 30 years later, would almost wipe out the Lakota nation.

I've had attorneys call me and say, "I'm doing this deed check, and the first name on here is Pecaut. It's got to be related to you." I'd say, "Yeah, that was my great-great-grandfather." He settled in Covington, Nebraska. Covington is where the Goodwill camp is located. That camp is where our local New Warrior Trainings are held for MKP. So there is all this energy in one place.

About eight years ago, we had a New Warrior Training at the Goodwill Camp where Chief Mel Lonehill, of the Pine Ridge Reservation, came down with seven of his men. It was the first time a group of Lakota men had participated in our weekend.

In MKP nationally, there was a lot of nervous energy and concern that it go well. We didn't want to offend. Nobody knew what would happen. Chief Lonehill trusted us, or he wouldn't have brought his men to the training. Still, we were nervous.

While he'd never done the New Warrior Training weekend, he and I had built a relationship over the years. MKP men had gone up to the reservation, sat in sweat lodges, and participated in sun dances.

I staffed the event. I wasn't sure how concerned I should be. I thought, "They're men. We're men. We'll figure this out." But I didn't know.

I remember the first young man from the reservation who walked through the door. He had hate steaming off him. I sensed that if I had gone up and pushed him, he would have taken my head off. He was seething.

While it was intense, we waded in and started going through the process. As the weekend progressed, tensions slowly relieved. Men came to understand themselves and one another at a deeper level.

The weekend was transformative. On the last morning, they sang us a Lakota friendship song. Everyone was crying. We started in a place of confusion and fear. By Sunday, we were brothers. The same man who was initially steaming hugged everyone on the staff.

It was beautiful. That experience deepened my belief in this work. We can be bumbling and unsure. But if we're genuine and follow the tried-and-true processes, it will work anyway.

After the weekend, a group of men, including myself, took a trip to the reservation. The idea was that we would sit with these men, share our tools, and learn from them. It would deepen the connection and understanding for all involved.

When I went up there, I expected some poverty and struggle, but I had no idea of the obstacles they faced—drugs, alcoholism, gangs, rape, violence, poverty, and turf wars. It was a sobering wake-up call for me about how bad and hopeless things can get. I had no clue what to do. Humbled, I went home and wondered, "What would it take to heal?"

Dallas Chief Eagle did the weekend five years ago in Colorado. Dallas has a degree in counseling. He has traveled all over the world as a hoop dancer, so he's a man of the world and a man of the people. He understands how things work in both worlds.

Dallas was excited about the idea of integrating MKP tools in his culture after he did his New Warrior Training weekend. He saw that MKP helps men change from the inside out and that it would work for his people.

Dallas and I staffed the next weekend. We were on the same team for some activities, and we bonded. I love him. He's an amazing visionary. He's a deep, open, soulful, brilliant man. As time went on, he kept bringing men to the weekends. About 30 to 40 native men have now been initiated.

He also had a vision of creating trainings in Pine Ridge. So he renovated a barn and started doing the circles we do but in a Lakota way. They integrated the MKP tools and processes with Lakota rituals and songs. For example, it's not uncommon for grief and sadness to come up in this process. The Lakota added their process to this work called

"The Wiping of the Tears" ceremony. It worked beautifully. In this way, he was able to begin bridging these two cultures.

After doing circles for a few years, he was ready to start hosting trainings on the reservation. In 2014, he hosted a Boys to Men training (for boys ages 12 to 17), a couples workshop, and an MKP-inspired warrior training. The warrior training, in particular, was fascinating. The elders added a sense of spirit and ritual and connected it to their traditions, ceremonies, and history.

As if this weren't enough, Dallas' biggest vision is to heal genocide throughout the world. He has a dream of building a genocide museum and a healing center for people to gather from all over the world to heal and learn.

American culture is in total denial about the genocide that we, as a group, perpetrated centuries ago. There's a deep shadow. For me, the shift is seeing how I can own my part in what was done and promote positive change by showing up and supporting a visionary like Dallas. That's the contribution I can make.

I'm aware that my great-great-grandfather played a role in settling the West, which set the stage for genocide, broken treaties, and the cultural destruction of the Plains natives. Now, 165 years later, here I am working with Dallas to heal those wounds. The elders, Dallas, and his wife Becky now call their friends at MKP their allies.

Dallas first presented the idea that the men of MKP were allies at a regional MKP meeting in 2013. It was an electrifying moment. We had about 30 men in a circle representing all the local communities of our Central Plains MKP region. When it was Dallas' turn, he spoke with thoughtful precision. No words were wasted. He said, "150 years ago we had allies. The Lakota made alliances with the Cheyenne, the Arapaho, and other tribes. Then the U.S. government came in, and we haven't had allies since. . . . until now. You men are our allies." There was silence as the impact of his words reverberated through the room. In that moment, Dallas transformed the relationship.

Dallas' father-in-law, Chubbs Thunder Hawk, a descendant of Sitting Bull, later shared with us the history of how those alliances came about and the story of how the Seven Council Fires would gather for the benefit of the people.

We decided to plan a "Making of Allies" ceremony on the reservation, where the elders and native community would gather with leaders from MKP and claim this alliance in ritual space.

Eighteen months later, the time had come. On March 14, 2015, a "Hunka," or "Making of Allies" ceremony, was held at the All Nations

Training Center at Pine Ridge. While I will give it words, words cannot adequately express the beauty, mystery, and power of the experience.

Let's start with the buffalo, which is the most sacred of animals to the Lakota, as they once depended on it for their very survival. On the day of the ceremony, a buffalo showed up. Simply amazing! (Most likely it had escaped from some local ranch. Once they escape, they cannot be returned since they'll teach the others how to escape.) The morning's agenda was promptly dropped, and all attention turned toward the buffalo. Dallas and the elders received permission to sacrifice the buffalo from the farmer as part of a ritual. Those of us in attendance were allowed to witness and participate. It was an incredible experience. It was seen as a blessing from the spirit world on what was about to transpire.

Chubbs, Dallas, and Becky would sign a Declaration of Alliance on behalf of the Indigenous Men and Women's Oyate* of Pine Ridge. Robert Powell (MKP Chair), Julien Devereux (MKP Chair-Elect), and Jon Levitt, (MKP Finance Chair) would represent MKP USA.

A MKP member, Filmmaker Frederick Marx, who created the Oscar-nominated documentary *Hoop Dreams*, came to document the event. Marx is passionate about healing youth through culturally appropriate rites of passage and noted that this was "right in my wheelhouse."

While a document was signed, what was done and said from the heart in ritual space was far more meaningful. The understanding was that this alliance was not so much an event as a milestone in building a new path toward healing—built with accountability, trust, and responsibility for our peoples. By sharing so intimately their ways with us, they were teaching us what it means to be allies. To grow into a relationship of trust with these beautiful people who suffered genocide, broken promises, and cultural destruction over the last 150 years is deeply humbling. I am in awe of their generosity of spirit.

I was so glad that Kay, my son Charlie, and my good friend David Bauerly were in the room to share this experience. Bauerly, a long-time leader in MKP, had been asked to lead a basic staff training for the native men who had already been initiated. However, with the buffalo showing up, there would be no time for that. It was powerful for me to share this experience with Kay and Charlie and to engage in healing work as a family. I was impressed how the Lakota circle includes the whole community—elders, women, children. All are invited in.

The relationship with Pine Ridge and MKP has long been built on personal friendships. Now the relationship has matured to the cultural

---

* *Oyate* means community.

and institutional level as well. We are allies. There is a weight of responsibility to honor this commitment, supporting the Oyate as they build their new path with healing from the inside out. There is a joy, too, of being shoulder to shoulder in mission.

Though I continue to support the alliance financially and work together to build enduring institutions, for me the simple presence and action in honor of Dallas Chief Eagle's vision is the most meaningful contribution I can make.

What type of impact could be bigger than healing the wounds of genocide?

ACTION STEPS:
PART THREE

Here is a distilled down summary of all the actions you can now take that you've read and understood what came before:

The impact we can make with our giving is 10 times what we think it is. There's a step change available to you if you grow your own capacities and awareness around giving and money.

You may wonder, "How much should I give?" The answer is always, "Start where you are. Do what works for you. The teaching will unfold naturally."

Bill Gates gave the Harvard commencement speech in 2005. In his speech, he said that he believes there's no shortage of compassion in the world. People care. What's stopping them is complexity. They just don't know what to do.

While where I ended up may seem intimidating, remember that I started with a dime in church on Sunday. If writing a check to United Way gives you satisfaction and makes a difference in your community, great. If time goes on and you feel a little dissatisfied and want to be a little more direct in your impact, good—you're ready for another step. Each person has to choose his or her own way and see where it unfolds.

I went from a collection plate, to tithing, to microlending, to a large gift, to helping develop a regional organization, to helping save a national organization, to hosting cross-cultural trainings, to developing alliances, to working on healing genocide.

Start where you are. There's nowhere else to start. See where your giving adventure takes you.

PROCEEDS:
HEALING THE WOUNDS
OF GENOCIDE

100% of the profits from this book will go toward healing the wounds of genocide by contributing to the All Nations Training Center at the Pine Ridge Reservation.

Dallas Chief Eagle and I created the Indigenous Men and Women's Oyate Training Fund to support this work. We greatly appreciate that MKP USA has agreed to administer the fund so all contributions are tax deductible.

Go to www.mkpusa.org/oyate to make a donation and to follow the progress of the All Nations Training Center and the Tatanka Alliance.

ACKNOWLEDGMENTS

I want to express my gratitude to Austin Pierce for having the vision to see the possibility of this book and inspiring me to write it and turn it from an idea into a reality. I couldn't have done it without you, Austin.

Appreciation to Davidson Wissing for being the listening foil that helped the book unfold through all those podcasts. Thanks, Davidson, for your curiosity and intellectual wonder.

Thanks also to our clients, who have helped me refine these ideas over the years. The last couple of decades have brought plenty of ups and downs, and you've had the patience to stay the course. In addition, you have read our newsletters over the years. You have let me know what works and makes sense and what doesn't. We so appreciate these long relationships and friendships.

Thanks to Shelby Pierce, my assistant, who actually started this whole thing by introducing me to Austin. She supports me each and every work day through managing my schedule, helping me with technology, information, communication, and her ebullient spirit.

Thanks also to Gayle Rupp, our long-time administrator at Pecaut & Company, for keeping things running smoothly. She brings a sunny disposition to handling the many details required to running a registered investment advisory firm. We have a great team at work and I appreciate their support day in and day out.

I definitely want to thank my partner Corey Wrenn, who always has believed in me, especially when I didn't believe in me. His support has been invaluable throughout my career, and he was totally supportive of the time and effort and resources that have been put into making this book.

Great gratitude to my friend, Dan Boyle. We met at a Berkshire Hathaway meeting nearly thirty years ago, and he has been a great friend and encourager ever since. He was the first to suggest I write this book.

I want to thank the early beta readers: Amber Hodges, Brenda Lussier, Corey Wrenn, David Aycock, Dan Boyle, Deb Dykstra, Dick McCormick, Frank Franciscovich, Helen Burstyn, Joel Wittenberg, John Pecaut, Judith Higgs, Mark Hantla, Melanie Arnold, Phil McLaughlin, Rob Roy, and Robert Meis. Thank you for reviewing an ugly draft of this book. Your feedback made it far better. I hope you're proud to be a part of it. I'm deeply grateful to all of you.

Deep gratitude to my parents, Dick and Dottie, who taught me so many life lessons and created an environment of love and curiosity for our family to grow in. While they're no longer alive, their voices of teaching and encouragement still ring in my head.

Thanks go to my children, John, Charlie, and Danielle, who have helped me grow in a thousand ways. One of their greatest lessons for me is that I always thought what I wanted was for them to be happy. Not quite. What I see now is that what I really always wanted was for them to take 100% responsibility for their lives. And they have. What a gift. It's for their generation that this book primarily is written.

Most of all, great love and thanks to my wife, Kay, my high school sweetheart and greatest teacher. She has loved me and supported me throughout. She doesn't care much for money. She does care that I show up with integrity, generosity, and love. Thanks, hon. I'm still learning . . .

APPENDIX:
FURTHER READING

The Intelligent Investor by Benjamin Graham

Influence: The Psychology of Persuasion by Robert B. Cialdini

Filters Against Folly: How To Survive Despite Economists, Ecologists, and the Merely Eloquent by Garrett Hardin

The Interpretation of Financial Statements by Benjamin Graham and Charles McGoldrick

Financial Statement Analysis, A Practitioner's Guide by Martin Fridson and Fernando Alvarez

Security Analysis by Benjamin Graham

PECAUT & COMPANY

Pecaut & Company is a federally registered investment advisor. If you would like more information about our services, you may contact us at:

Pecaut & Company
401 Douglas Street, Suite 415
Sioux City, IA 51101

712-252-3268
800-779-7326

www.pecautandcompany.com

www.ingramcontent.com/pod-product-compliance
Lightning Source LLC
Chambersburg PA
CBHW022041190326
41520CB00008B/677